# Down the Rivers on a Chainsaw

### Logs of the Travels of the Pleasure Craft, the *Saundra Kay*

## BJ Gillum

2$^{nd}$ edition
Published 2016

ISBN:       1541378385
ISBN 13: 9781541378384

Published by
Port Gillum Press
115 Indian Mound Lane
Rockwood, Tennessee 37854
*bjgillum@comcast.net*

In association with
GJ Publishing
*www.neilans.com*

# Acknowledgements

- ⚓ Saundra for the loving support
- ⚓ Steve for his help and companionship
- ⚓ Doc and Jan Jacobs for their seamanship and good advice
- ⚓ The Greene Cove Yacht Club gang for their encouragement:

Paul and Beverly Buckles
Bob and Jan Ditmar
Deacon and Marlene Koenig
Jerry and Donna McGinnis
Tom and Sue Whyard and son, Robbie

# CONTENTS

# Dedicated to

Saundra Kay Gillum
January 19, 1942 ... June 5, 2016

# Preface

Since I was a small boy on a farm in Kentucky water has fascinated me. For me it was the easiest form of entertainment whether wading, trying to learn to swim, diving from limbs or fishing with homemade hooks and string tied to a willow pole. Creeks were always mysterious places to explore. Strange and interesting animals lived in the water and along and under the banks. It was alive and filled with mystery for me. As I grew older and my world expanded my experience with water never included any great voyages of exploration as I had dreamed of as a boy, but I never lost the urge to take a long boat trip someday.

A stint in the Marine Corp gave me the opportunity to see the Pacific Ocean first hand on a troop carrier from San Diego to Japan and Japan to the Philippine Islands. This wide expanse of water with no shoreline didn't satisfy my appetite for travel by boat.

In the late sixties a trip across Lake Erie from Cleveland,

Ohio to Point Pelee, Canada in a twin outboard during a "small craft warning" storm condition taught me the value of preparation and the wisdom of following boating safety rules.

A 1993 boat show in Pittsburg, PA was the real beginning of my boating story. A Bayliner Boat dealer there had a boat to sell which my wife, Saundra, and I really liked. We bought the boat and docked her sixty-five miles up the Monongahela River at Millsboro, PA. We spent a lot of time there and met a wonderful group of boaters who loved to spend their spare time on or around water. Among them were Doc and Jan Jacobs; he is a Professor of English Literature and Jan is a former school teacher who works in a Doctor's office. They own a 21 foot Bayliner cruiser and just took delivery on a 54 foot Gibson houseboat.

In March 1994 I took early retirement from my job of 35 years with the Western Electric Company, by then called AT&T Technologies and later changed to Lucent Technologies. I was fifty-five years old last year and we had purchased our "retirement lot" near Kingston, Tennessee on Watts Bar Lake, a TVA lake on the Tennessee River. We had a local builder construct a dock on the site and had it powered from a temporary power pole.

Doc and Jan agreed to accompany us since they were interested in exploring the river systems and hadn't been down the Ohio to Paducah, Kentucky and never on the Tennessee River. They were experienced boaters and Coast Guard Auxiliary Officers.

We obtained river charts, verified boat facilities along the route by phone, made a float plan and schedule, shipped furniture and household belongings to a temporary storage near our destination and prepared our boats for an eighteen day cruise.

A farewell dinner with our boating friends and we were ready to depart on our dream cruise on July 12, 1994, or so we thought.

This is my story of that adventure.

*Millsboro, Pennsylvania to Kingston, Tennessee*

⚓ Total mileage (approximate): 1,660 miles
⚓ Lockages:        30
⚓ Travel time:    18 days
⚓ Departure:      July 12, 1994

# Boats on the Cruise

The *Saundra Kay* - 25 foot Bayliner Sierra 2556
Command Bridge cabin cruiser
w/flying bridge and Bimini top
Powered by 7.4L Mercruiser I/O w/Bravo 2 Outdrive
Fuel- Gasoline (102 gallon capacity)
Range - 100 miles

*Crew*
Captain: Bill Gillum
First Mate: Saundra Gillum
Able Bodied Seaman: Steve Grant

The *Roamer* - 21 foot Bayliner cuddy cabin cruiser,
open bridge with canvas cover
Powered by Volvo I/O
Fuel - Gasoline (55 gallon)
Range - 170 miles

*Crew*
Captain: Allan "Doc" Jacobs
First Mate: Jan Jacobs

# Routes Followed:

## Monongahela River:
Greene Cove Yacht Club to Pittsburgh, Pennsylvania

## Ohio river:
Pittsburgh, Pennsylvania to Paducah, Kentucky
(22 mile side trip on Kentucky River)

## Cumberland River
Paducah, Kentucky to Kentucky Lake

## Tennessee River
Kingston, Tennessee

*******

Shoreline boundaries include:
Pennsylvania
West Virginia
Ohio
Kentucky
Indiana
Illinois
Tennessee
Mississippi

*******

*Notes:*
L  =  left bank down bound
R  = right bank down bound

# Cruising the Rivers

## The Saundra Kay

## Log One

Millsboro, Pennsylvania to Kingston, Tennessee

July 12, 1994 to July 30, 1994

July 11, 1994 Monday

## Preparations for the cruise

Greene Cove Yacht Club
Millsboro, PA

This morning broke slowly; the sun burned its way through a thick blanket of fog after a cool night. By 8:15 a.m. sunlight appeared to be winning the struggle.

Jan Jacobs is at home in Uniontown, PA doing the last minute things that must be done before we depart. Grass has to be mowed, banking has to be done and a host of other chores. Doc's boat, *Roamer*, a 21 foot Bayliner has been taken to a repair facility to have final adjustments made but concern remains in his eyes. An overloaded boat, straining to get up and on plane, will not be able to last 1,660 miles. The stubborn four cylinder Volvo remains a mystery and is difficult to tune but when she is properly adjusted she runs smooth and steady. We are hoping she will be ready to leave on the original schedule of 8:00 a.m. July, 12th.

Today Deacon Koenig is driving me to the Greene County Airport in Waynesburg to meet Steve Grant, my brother-in-law. He is flying in from Jackson, Ohio with a friend who is a pilot. Their Piper Cub is scheduled to arrive between 9 a.m. and 10 a.m. this morning. Steve will have only one day to get acquainted with the boat and prepare for our 18 day cruise. Steve arrived at 12 noon. He explained that due to a last minute intestinal distress the original pilot couldn't fly and he had to arrange for a substitute pilot.

We had lunch at the airport with Mark Hamel, the pilot, Steve and his son, Brad, then drove to Greene Cove Yacht Club. We filled our tanks with fuel and packed our ice chest/live well with frozen food, ice and drinks. We were ready to shove off in the morning. Deacon and Marlene Koenig were going to see us off and then return to their home to have work done on their new "Florida" room.

At 3:30 p.m. Doc finally got *Roamer* back from Engle's Marina repair facility. He called Jan and said, "*Roamer's* fixed and we can make the trip; get the last things together and I'll soon be home with the trailer."

6:30 p.m. arrived - no Doc. The First Mate, Jan, became very concerned. At 7 p.m. Doc came down the street with his Bronco and boat trailer which are to be left at his home in case Kurt, the Jacobs' son, needs to come to their rescue. Their neighbors are waiting to bring them back to the marina as they don't want to leave their car parked at the Marina while they are away. As Phil and Mildred left the marina with Doc's car, Jan asked Doc where he put the ice chest for *Roamer* - it was still in the Bronco at their home! As the taillights turn toward Le Mont Furnace, Jan looked around. None of the five of us had a car to rescue the ice chest. Jan convinced Marlene to make the hour and a half trip. By 10:30 p.m. the ice chest has been rescued thanks to Marlene.

## July 12, 1994 Tuesday

Greene Cove Yacht Club, Millsboro, Pennsylvania
to
Beaver River
Ohio River, Mile 25.4R

At 8:45 a.m. we departed Greene Cove in a brisk summer breeze. We were barely under way when Doc radioed that he was returning to the Marina; Roamer was having a problem getting up on plane. When we got to their boat slip Jan thought there was too much weight aboard so she started taking extra blankets, clothes, and gear off Roamer and storing them aboard their Houseboat, Doc's Delight. Beer, a box of canned goods and the rescued ice chest were stowed aboard the *Saundra Kay*. Midway through the off- loading of supplies the men noticed a problem with the trim tabs on Roamer. We tightened the hydraulic fluid line clamp, refilled the reservoir and departed again at 11 a.m. Again, problems with the trim tabs caused a delay. We returned to the Cove where Doc replaced the hydraulic pump unit with a new unit on the port side trim tab. Another attempt to leave was made before another leak in the hose connection was detected. We returned to the Cove's fuel dock where we used a socket wrench to tighten two new hose clamps on the offending hose. We finally left at 12 noon and were able to continue with Doc not fully confident that Roamer was running properly. He decided to continue the cruise with the understanding that he had the option to return if his boat began to perform poorly again.

The delays caused us to have a rather long first day since we had planned to cruise six locks and ninety-five miles. But with amazing luck at the locks, we were able to keep to our first day's schedule. That evening at The Captains Quarters Marina was very pleasant. We met the owners and some of the boating members there. For dinner we had kielbasa, potato salad, sauerkraut and copper pennies (carrot salad).

## July 13, 1994 Wednesday

Beaver River
Ohio River, mile 25.4R
to
Sistersville Boat Club
Ohio River, Mile 136.5L

Again we had incredible luck with locking through the four locks on our cruising schedule today. The 111.1 miles were covered with dispatch and we arrived at Sistersville in the early evening. We toured the points of interest including a historic oil well and watched a ferry operating across the Ohio River. The owners of the Sistersville Boat Club invited us aboard their houseboat where they live much of the time. They were justifiably proud of their hospitality to transient boaters; we felt right at home.

During the evening we were treated to the spectacular sight of the Mississippi Queen stern-wheel paddle boat as she passed headed upstream. Her lights made her appear as large as a floating city and her wake rocked the moored boats and the floating docks handily.

### July 14, 1994 Thursday

Sistersville Boat Club
Ohio River, Mile 136.5L
to
Marietta Harbor
Ohio River, Mile 173R

Today, Thursday July 14, 1994 the morning broke with low, gray clouds.

Rain from the night before puddled on wet dock boards. The weather for today is supposed to be rainy too with the possibility of thunder showers. Our next destination is Marietta, Ohio located at the mouth of the Muskingum River. There is one lock on this stretch of river and the total run is only 36.5 miles. After breakfast and coffee a conference is held and the decision is made to proceed to our next destination.

A light rain was falling as we departed Sistersville, West Virginia at 9:30 a.m. *Roamer* took the lead since the weather conditions were degrading rapidly and fog began to appear over the water. The *Saundra Kay* developed problems with

VHF radio channel 16. Visibility decreased and we slowed to nearly idle speed for about forty-five minutes. A break in the fog gave us a chance to maintain a higher speed and we proceeded to Marietta at normal cruising speed.

We arrived at our destination at 12:10 p.m. Fuel was taken aboard and lunch was enjoyed by the crew of the *Saundra Kay*. *Roamer's* crew had lunched during the last leg of the run from the lock.

A walking tour of Marietta, Ohio was very enjoyable although rain did reappear in the form of gentle showers. We made a trip to a doughnut shop and went to a grocery store and beer barn for supplies. Saundra visited a hairdresser who promised to "make her beautiful." We made reservations for dinner at 7 p.m. at the Lafayette Hotel overlooking the Ohio River.

Dinner was wonderful and the atmosphere was unmatched. We finally retired to our boats and slept well, hoping to awake in the morning to better weather.

# July 15, 1994 Friday

Marietta, Ohio
Ohio River, Mile 173R
to
Gallipolis, Ohio
Ohio River, Mile 270R

The crews were awake early and enjoying coffee on the dock at Marietta by 6:30 a.m. The sky was overcast with low, hazy clouds or fog. Before we could depart, the men dashed off to the Beer Barn for ice and Jan went back to the Lafayette Hotel in hopes of retrieving her purse holder.

We cast off and headed down the river. The *Saundra Kay* lingered momentarily by Blennerhassett Island to view the Mansion and grounds through binoculars.

*Roamer* continued and *Saundra Kay* caught up with her in a few minutes.

The barges we encountered on this section of river were larger than we had encountered on previous legs of the cruise. We gave them wide berth when necessary and tried to take the most advantageous passing approach to conserve fuel.

Wind began to generate wave conditions which, in the longer stretches became twelve inch chop with occasional white caps. The steady wind, approximately ten to fifteen miles an hour, brought a welcome relief from the heat of the previous day.

I was piloting the *Saundra Kay* until the Belleville Lock was behind us at 10:40 a.m. when Saundra took the wheel. The waves and wind were steady until we reached Racine Lock and Dam at Ohio River Mile 238.

We decided to proceed to Gallipolis without taking on fuel and I took the helm to get us through the lock. Inside the lock, the wind suddenly began to increase as I approached the floating locking bitt. My reaction was not quick enough to keep us from forcefully striking the lock wall with our bow rail. Fortunately the lock wall and our bow rail were only scratched.

Steve chose not to take his turn at the helm for the last leg of this run so I kept the wheel.

The steady wind and waves continued and our increased fuel consumption rate caused me to maintain the most fuel efficient speed. Radio contact was maintained with *Roamer* and the distance between our boats gradually increased.

Just before we reached the Gallipolis Boat Club we lost radio contact with *Roamer*. We had extended our lead to six miles by that time so we slowed to idle speed and moved to the side of the channel to wait until radio contact could be restored. We decided to wait for five minutes and if contact was not made the *Saundra Kay* would backtrack to find *Roamer*. Before that time elapsed *Roamer* rounded a bend and contacted us by radio.

We continued to the mouth of the Chickamauga Creek and waited for *Roamer* to come into view again then proceeded into the harbor and tied up at the fuel dock.

Our fuel gauge read "Empty" but we required only eighty-two gallons to fill up. That means, riding at rest, we have twenty gallons of fuel left in our tank when the fuel gauge first registers "Empty." *Roamer* ran aground while she was attempting to dock in her assigned slip. Doc used his outdrive to push out of the mud and moored *Roamer* in a different slip.

*Saundra Kay* raised her outdrive to avoid a similar fate and, with the help of Doc and Jan, left the fuel dock and tied up at her slip without any problem.

Doc expressed his disapproval of my leaving too much distance between our boats resulting in the loss of radio contact. I agreed that it was not a good practice, offered my apology for my error and promised to stay closer in the future. It was not my intention to cause concern by being out of radio range. Closer attention to fuel management and planning should assure that similar situations won't happen again.

We were enjoying evening refreshments when the sky decided to give up her wind and water and added some lightning and thunder just to remind us who is boss. The rain was refreshingly cooling and Doc began frolicking about in his bathing suit to take advantage of nature's shower. We all showered.

Saundra provided the main course for dinner; a delicious beef stew. Jan questioned whether Saundra had prayed for rain to cool things down so that we could enjoy this hot dish. Jan provided delicious hors d'oeuvres and apple pie for dessert. Steve brought the ice cream from the local grocery for the A La Mode. Both crews retired for the night at about ten thirty; thankful for the cool night air.

## July 16, 1994 Saturday

Gallipolis, Ohio
Ohio River, Mile 270R
to
Shawnee State Park Marina
Ohio River, Mile 363R

Today, Saturday, the fifth day of the trip dawned foggy and threatening. After breakfast and the usual morning preparations it was decided that the weather was too bad to begin today's cruise at 8:00 a.m. as planned. By 10:05 a.m. both boats left their slips at Gallipolis Boat Club. The cooling effect of the rain of the previous evening was still felt as our boats planed out and reached cruising speed.

At Ohio River Mile 308L we stopped for fuel at the Huntington, West Virginia Yacht Club. Doc was removing the gas "fill" cap from Roamer when suddenly the cap assumed the ability to travel on its own power and flung itself into the Ohio River. To doc's amazement, the plastic retaining ring had no effect on the trajectory of the speeding missile and it fell to the bottom of the river. Not to be outdone by a mechanical device, Doc pondered the situation carefully and decided that the current use of the boat hook handle should be expanded. He took his trusty knife, removed the last inch and a half of the plastic handle, fitted it with a restraining safety string, and inserted it into the gaping hole. Alas, man's inventiveness wins the day!

As the day progressed the weather improved until by early afternoon bright sunlight had returned. We arrived in the Shawnee State Park Marina and tied up. Soon we were visited by Glenna and Lafayette (Lafe) Boggs, Jr., my sister and brother-in-law, from Sandy Hook, Kentucky. They brought green beans, potatoes and cabbage, corn bread and apple cobbler. We all shared the meal while we visited with them. Soon Steve's son, Brad, and daughter, Cathy stopped by with Cathy's friends Crystal and Liza. We visited for about an hour and when they left we just relaxed and enjoyed the cool evening at the boats.

Doc and Jan Jacobs relaxing on *The Roamer*
At the Shawnee State Park Marina

## July 17, 1994 Sunday

Shawnee State Park Marina
Ohio River, Mile 363R
to
Four Seasons Marina, Cincinnati, Ohio
Ohio River, Mile 463R

At 6:15 a.m. a dense fog covered the marina. The still, cool air was comfortable. Occasionally a call from a sentinel crow in the treetops nearby echoed across the small cove below. Soon, faces began to appear in the windows of the boat cabins and the smell of brewing coffee filled the air.

Jan arose from an interrupted sleep and asked who was talking at four in the morning. That was my cue to blame Steve's ham radio. Steve denied responsibility and pointed out that he must turn it off before it goes on charge at night. It might be that the VHF radio was not turned off last night from the bridge? I was caught!

The fog began to lift at 9:11 a.m. and the crews are restless and anxious to prepare to shove off. By 9:30 a.m. both boats have departed their slips and at 9:34 a.m. cruised past the first day mark of the run at mile 363.5 on the Ohio River. The cruising was excellent with Saundra and Steve on the flying bridge.

At Meldahl Lock we encountered a slight delay, and upon entering we were rocked by a small boat's wake. As we left the lock, the small boat sped toward the gates and

15

again her wake rocked our boats. This rude and unsafe act did not go unnoticed by Jan who took extreme verbal exception to their unsafe behavior.

At approximately 2:56 p.m. Doc reported that Roamer's engine had backfired and developed a noticeable decline in top end engine RPM, and that a loud noise could be heard. He suspected the timing belt had slipped due to the rough water we had encountered. Also, a fuel problem was possible since we had just refueled. At about the same time we were met by hordes of Sunday afternoon pleasure boaters. Due to the congestion and wakes the rest of the run to the Four Seasons Marina at Ohio River Mile 463R was very unpleasant. We arrived frustrated but safe at 4:08 p.m.

The *Saundra Kay* took on fuel and Roamer requested information about mechanics and repairs before we decided to confirm our overnight plans. We decided to stay in Four Seasons Marina as planned and get repairs on Monday.

The day's cruising had been excellent with the exception of the congestion caused by the large number of Sunday boaters.

The ladies decided to save money and use some of the provisions we had in our cooler. Dinner was served after Jan had laundered Roamer's wash and while Saundra was finishing her rather large laundry load. Dinner was chili, green beans, buttered rolls heated in the microwave, sliced onion, potatoes in cooked cabbage with apple cobbler heated in the microwave for dessert. The original twenty-five pound block of ice still remains in the cooler (Sunday 8 p.m.) and is now the size of a softball. This proves the cooler is okay and that solid blocks of ice are the longest lasting ice for coolers. This block has lasted for five days.

# July 18, 1994 Monday

*- Rescheduled-*
Four seasons Marina - Cincinnati, Ohio
to
Pier 99 - Warsaw, KY

Rain during the night cleared the skies and lowered the temperature. *Roamer* is waiting for a mechanic to show at about noon today. At 10 a.m. *Roamer* blew an on board fuse while using their vacuum cleaner. A search is now underway to locate the elusive blown fuse. The *Saundra Kay* crew is using the time to reorganize and prepare for the next leg of the cruise. Hopefully we will all be able to continue to Pier 99 later today.

During our stay Doc was able to find two gas filler caps to replace the lost cap and have a spare on board. He and Steve managed to install a bypass circuit for the vacuum cleaner outlet. This is also the outlet for the cabin fan which is a necessity on this trip!

The mechanic looked at *Roamer's* engine and determined that a water filter was clogged with mud from the Gallipolis grounding and a possible problem with fuel could have caused the lower RPM reading. A test run helped to verify that 4,200 RPM is attainable. The mechanic is scheduled to return tomorrow morning to finish his job.

Meanwhile the swimming pool is too inviting and I cannot resist. In mid-afternoon I tried the pool and found it to be wonderfully pleasant. I returned to the boats and the rest of the crew decided to try the pool too. We all donned bathing suits, slathered our bodies with suntan lotion and spent a couple of hours in the pool.

Reluctantly, we returned to the boats and the ladies began to prepare dinner.

I mentioned to Doc that there was an oily sheen on the water behind *Roamer's* trim tabs. He decided to check them out. On the first try, the trim tab on the port side squirted hydraulic oil onto the swim platform. So, while dinner was being prepared, the three men replaced the split hose with a new hose and new hose clamps. Hopefully this will end the trouble with the stubborn trim tabs.

Dinner was served at about 8:30 p.m. and was a delightful repast of four salads; Dijon potato salad, garden salad with croutons, copper pennies (carrots), and sour creamed cucumbers with onions. The main course was hot dogs and kielbasa sandwiches. Dessert was marbled cake with white icing but nobody admitted they had a birthday today!

The evening was pleasant and cool with an expected temperature of sixty-two degrees for the low temperature tonight; a fair and sunny day is predicted for tomorrow.

# July 19, 1994 Tuesday

Four Seasons Marina, Cincinnati, Ohio
Ohio River, Mile 463R
to
Pier 99 Marina, Warsaw, Kentucky
Ohio River, Mile 530.5L

Today is a bright, sunny morning with almost no fog. A few puffy white clouds soon dissipate in the bright morning sun. I take a fast stroll around the marina while the mechanic completes his work on *Roamer*. Doc appears eager to continue the journey and suggests that he go to a marina across the Ohio River to refuel while we complete preparations on the *Saundra Kay*. We shove off at about 9:45 a.m. and meet *Roamer* at 10 a.m. Unfortunately the staff of the Waterfront Marina had shifted into their snail's pace and we waited for about an hour before anyone came to sell gas and supplies. Only through the efforts of Saundra was our need recognized. We finally departed with ice and fuel fully stocked.

After cruising on the beautiful Ohio River past Cincinnati and by The Mississippi Queen moored at Riverfront Stadium and the Spirit of America moored downstream, we stopped at Aurora, Indiana to restock our galley. Saundra and Jan went ashore for provisions while we men remained with the boats at the fuel dock to top off the fuel tanks. It became apparent that this was an unusual stop when the men noticed the fuel pumps were not manned but were "womaned" by the most delightful, scantily clad young ladies. Doc immediately topped his tank off with a massive purchase of $5.00. I suspect it was so that he could feast his sunbaked eyes on these luscious creatures. But, I could be wrong. Steve began buying things I know his doctor would not approve and I even purchased a fifty pound block of ice. Luckily the ladies returned before serious damage was done to our budgets.

We proceeded downstream with *Roamer* suddenly traveling at an extraordinarily rapid pace. That engine had apparently come to life! Alas, soon he stopped just as suddenly, announcing that the engine coughed (or had it farted?), and after a short consultation we again resumed the cruise. This was repeated after another fifteen miles. We made it into the Pier 99 lagoon at about 3:15 p.m. We were met by very friendly people who assisted us by calling Markland Lock for locking information. We were assigned covered slips and assisted into them.

Doc inspected R*oamer's engine* and noticed that a plug was missing from the metal valve cover assembly. He formed a plug from aluminum foil from *Saundra Kay*'s galley and placed it in the hole. He then started the engine to test the device, not realizing that he had left the throttle in the full forward position. The resulting horrendous noise caused by the fully revving engine may have caused his hasty trip to "check out the bathrooms and showers."

Saundra and Jan prepared a dinner of Salisbury steak, sour creamed potatoes, garden salad and leftover cucumber salad. After dinner Jan decided to prepare the marinade for tomorrow's chuck steak. She was shaking the steak in the sauce to combine the juices with the flavors when suddenly the zip lock bag split and the marinade spilled over the transom of the *Saundra Kay* and across the swim platform. A swift squirt from a water hose removed the mess.

It should be noted that the temperature, in the shade, is 98 degrees.

If we had been on schedule we would have cleared the Markland Lock the day before its planned closing of the big lock for repairs. We all decided to get up at 4:30 - 5:00 a.m. to be underway at 6:00 a.m. as tomorrow is to be one of the longest legs of the trip. It will be 134.5 miles and nowhere to stop before Leavenworth, Indiana. We are getting into lonely, long stretches of the Ohio River.

## July 20, 1994 Wednesday

Pier 99 Marina, Warsaw, Kentucky
Ohio River, Mile 530L
to
Leavenworth, Indiana
Ohio River, Mile 664.5R

This is a difficult, long reach; it will be hot and wrought with concerns about locking through the Markland Locks which are under construction and have an estimated three hour delay.

Plans have been made to rise early and to approach the locks at approximately 7:00 a.m. in order to beat the expected traffic. We rise early and shove off as planned and when Doc contacts the lock master for lockage down-bound we are elated that we are instructed to proceed to the lock gates to be locked through. Thus, what could have been a very boring and hot delay has become a delightful early start.

The first leg is to the Kentucky River where we traverse the first five miles to the first lock and back. This lock is a pre-Civil War lock and is manually operated.

Louisville, Kentucky and the McAlpine Lock and Dam at mile 607L of the Ohio River are reached with no major incident.

Louisville is a beautiful city and the river water fountain in the center of the river is a sight to behold.

A slight misunderstanding at the entrance to the lock caused some concern but no real delay. The radio instructions from the lockmaster would not be clear to anyone who had never used these locks. And we were all required to wear life jackets in order to enter the lock.

We continued to our destination of the Port of Leavenworth Marina. The people there are very friendly and allowed us to use their picnic area and outdoor furniture. We used the barbecue grill from the *Saundra Kay* to cook the marinated chuck steak and had potatoes and bean salad as side dishes.

Note: This was another hot day for weary sailors - 95 Degrees!

The evening was not uneventful, however, as the pent up strain of extended travel was evidenced by an emotional outburst from myself directed toward Saundra. Saundra reacted by refusing to participate in dinner. Hurt feelings and worn nerves aggravated by river travel lead to the venting of human emotional strain. Tears, words of concern and soul searching followed. Human beings, under strain and stress, can be expected to act this way when thrust into close quarters or when forced to suddenly share important tasks and responsibilities without having time to fully adjust to individual styles and personality traits. It is unrealistic to suggest that people of strong will and conviction can change without a major motivating reason. As the evening wears on, maturity exerts itself and the healing process begins. Alas; humanity is justified and restored.

Note: At bedtime the temperature is 95 degrees.

During the night (3:30 a.m. to be precise) The Mississippi Queen passed our overnight dockage on her way downstream. Needless to say, the boats which were moored on the river side of the docks were severely rocked by her massive wakes. The boats seemed to rise and fall four feet or more with each wake. In our V births in the bow of the boat we felt the power of the waves as we were hurled off our bunks toward the overhead and felt weightless as we fell back to the bunk, only to be met by the rising bunk and again hurled skyward. The hulls of the boats were dashed against the floating docks with great noise and only the sturdy nylon lines and large bumpers saved us from serious damage. *This must be what it feels like to ride a bucking bronco*, I thought. No apparent damage was done to the boats that night, but I'm not so sure about the nerves of the crews.

# July 21, 1994 Thursday

Port of Leavenworth, Indiana
Ohio River, Mile 664.5R
to
Owensboro Marina, Owensboro, Kentucky
Ohio River Mile 756.5L

We slept late and slowly prepared to leave. This run is only ninety-two miles and one lock so we feel it will not be difficult. The morning was foggy but had changed to hazy conditions by 8:50 a.m. when we left. The river became more beautiful and scenic as we passed pastoral countryside. Cows lounged belly deep in the cooling water at rivers edge. Long pools of mirror smooth water were crossed with hardly a sensation of resistance. It was almost as if we were floating in the air just above the water's surface. Gradually the haze cleared somewhat and as we stopped to refuel just short of the Cannelton Lock at Ohio River mile 721R a short thunderstorm passed over us. We waited a few minutes, visited the grocery store, and discussed whether to lock through rather than wait for the possibility of another rainstorm to pass. My able bodied seaman and brother-in-law, Steve Grant, has been a student of weather and is generally considered to be something of an authority on that subject. "Steve, what do you think, is it over?" I asked. Steve studied the sky and appeared to be confident that the storm was over. "It looks good to me," he said. "Let's go!"

About half way across the mile or so to the locks the sky was split by a lightning bolt bright as a flash bulb! Suddenly I realized that we were about as exposed as we could get; sitting there on the flying bridge clinging to the shiny metal wheel! Only one thing to do - run like crazy for the locks! We made it to the lock gates, they opened and as we idled into the lock a gigantic thunder clap and lightning flash confirmed our doubt about the decision to lock through.

Committed now, we struggled to get in position before the storm got worse. The *Saundra Kay* made for the mid-point floating locking bitt but before we could get a line over the bitt a strong wind gust forced her away from the wall. We turned, still in the grasp of the wind, and made for the opposite wall. Hard reverse power to the prop pulled us off the wall before serious damage was done. Then a torrential rain set in and the engine stalled and quit. Helpless in the wind without power, she drifted backward toward the upstream gates. I made for the bridge to restart the engine because the keys were there and she could only be restarted with those keys. Blinded by gusting wind, lightning flashes and heavy, blowing rain I finally got the engine restarted. By now the boat was nearly against the lock gates and was being held off by Saundra and Steve using boat hooks as poles to push against the gates. We managed to nudge her forward and away from the gates to the first locking bitt where Steve secured her, in a downpour, with a line. It held! Steve stayed at his post through fifteen minutes of heavy rain, lightning and thunder. After the storm had lessened in intensity Saundra found our only umbrella and offered it to the totally drenched Steve. He laughed and declined the offer.

While the Saundra Kay was struggling with the wind she was not alone in her misery. Roamer's crew also had their hands full but managed to secure her before the full storm hit. They were not able to fully control her in the wind and as the lock emptied, she rode down the wall dragging her swim platform along the wall. Doc contacted the lockmaster and requested permission to remain in the lock until the storm subsided. The Lockmaster agreed, of course, and we left the lock about ten minutes after the gates opened.

The remaining thirty-five miles to Owensboro, Kentucky were on choppy water with brisk winds and cloudy skies. Some of the longer reaches were covered with twelve to eighteen inch chop and occasional white caps.

When we arrived in Owensboro Marina, Owensboro, Kentucky, Ohio River Mile 756.5L it was approximately 3:00 p.m. EDT (2:00 p.m. CDT). Owensboro has a riverfront park area just above the marina and is a clean, pleasant city. Doc and Jan took advantage of the nearby Executive Inn and registered there for a night off the boat. The *Saundra Kay* crew strolled along the waterfront and had an Italian dinner in the Pasta Plenty Restaurant.

Doc and Jan returned with a greeting card from Tom and Sue Whyard, They had mailed the card there in advance of the Jacobs' arrival. It was good to be reminded that we have friends who share our trip with us and remember us this way. We wish they could be here in person.

Since tomorrow's run is going to be very long (145.5 miles with two locks) we decide to weigh anchor at 7:00 a.m.

Note: Today marks the completion of the first half of this trip. So far we have traveled approximately 823 miles and have been on the rivers for nine days. We have lost only one day from our original float plan and that was due to concern over a possible mechanical failure of an engine.

## July 22, 1994 Friday

Owensboro, Kentucky
Ohio River, Mile 756.5L
to
Golconda, Illinois
Ohio River, Mile 902R

The Ohio River became more beautiful as we continued downstream. Many barges were met or passed and generally we handled them very well. A few gave us exceptional wakes to test our skills but Steve, our Captain for today, piloted us nearly all the way and managed to dispatch them with professionalism. All except one, which to our consternation, had us riding at the crest of her wake until we were listing at what seemed to be a critical angle. Since I was sitting at the lower helm I took immediate action in order to preserve the boat, her crew and the clean state of my underwear. I jammed the throttle forward to the limit and the *Saundra Kay* responded in her usual way by gulping large quantities of fuel and leaping forward at a high rate of speed. In what seemed only a week we were off the crest of the wake and in smooth water again. This tow was the "Sullivan" with 31 jumbo barges. Right behind her was a tow with 15 barges and a third tow. *Roamer* and her venerable Captain, Doc Jacobs, seemed to skim the wakes very well but reports by radio indicated that a healthy respect for towboat wakes was the order of the day.

Our lockages were very quick with the lockmasters preparing the locks as we approached. Breezes in the locks seem to be normal here. Again, we find ourselves bracing against strong persistent wind in the locks. After a brief consultation on the matter we all agreed that earthmover tires strapped to the sides of the boats would provide adequate protection.

We passed through long reaches of rough water with three foot swells and white caps causing some bumpy rides for the crews. Both Doc and Steve have been complaining of a condition which could best be described as anal compression or cheek dislocation. Steve suggested that "Donut" ring seats could be the answer but it was rejected out of hand because of the way they are associated with the dreaded "piles." During this stretch of rough water *Roamer* started having problems. Doc thought he was hitting air pockets but this later proved to be the beginning of *Roamer's* major mechanical problems.

We passed the Cave-in-the-Rock and viewed it only from the river. It certainly appeared that it would have been a perfect pirate hideout as historians claim. Maybe Pittsburgh should send her Pirates baseball team here to hide when they play poorly!

At 3:00 p.m. we tied up at the Golconda, Illinois Marina and filled our gas tanks. Covered slips with water and electric on excellent docks were made available to us. This facility is very high quality and is a friendly place, just off the river and up a canal. Our slip cost about twelve dollars and fuel is $1.44/5 per gallon for 89 octane. The showers were clean and locked and the privacy is good. Security is excellent and we feel completely comfortable and at ease here.

Joe and Joan, cousins of the Jacobs, joined us at the dock and we really enjoyed their company. Joan took Jan and Saundra to town to resupply our food and Saundra's water supply. Her bunk was almost empty of water jugs so it was the perfect time to resupply for the long trip up the Tennessee River. We had dinner on the *Saundra Kay* and Doc, Jan, Joe and Joan got all gussied up, "looked normal," and went to The Mansion for dinner.

## July 23, 1994 Saturday

Golconda, Illinois
Ohio River Mile 902R
to
Green Turtle Bay Marina, Grand Rivers, Kentucky
Barkley Lake Mile 31.8L

Today our crew slept late again, expecting a short run and an easy day. WRONG! We felt so confident that we would encounter no problems that by nine a.m. we had hardly done enough to be noticed. We were soon to be introduced to the fickle finger of fate.

At approximately 9:00 a.m. Doc suggested that we think about getting underway and proceeded to the fuel dock to get some ice cubes for his cooler. The *Saundra Kay* was to go to that same dock to meet *Roamer* and start down the Ohio River to Kentucky Lake by way of the Cumberland River and the Barkley Canal. When the *Saundra Kay* started her 7.4 Liter engine a strange noise came from the engine compartment. It could be described as a pulsating whine or vibrating screech whichever suits your mood. It was not a noise we were expecting to hear and it did not instill great confidence in us. We discussed our options:

1. Abandon ship and check into the nearest motel.
2. Blame everything on Steve, abandon ship and check into the nearest motel.
3. Pretend it didn't happen and ignore the noisy

screeching sound.

4. Check under the engine hatch to see whether we had acquired a small animal which has caught its tail under the fan belt.

5. Find a competent mechanic and have the engine checked.

We chose options 4 and 5. Doc radioed for a mechanic and we stayed in our slip and checked the engine compartment. Nothing seemed out of place and we could not determine what caused the noise.

The mechanic arrived after about forty-five minutes and looked at the engine. Meanwhile, *Roamer* had returned to her slip and her crew was waiting for the *Saundra Kay* to be made whole. The problem was soon identified as a galled distributor shaft housing assembly. Simply stated, it was messed up. The unit was taken to the shop, disassembled, inspected, lubricated and reinstalled. The noise was now virtually undetectable. We cast off at approximately 12:10 p.m. The morning was beautiful with puffy clouds in a blue sky.

A short run to the Smithland Lock was interrupted only by some pleasure boaters who managed to give us some unwelcome wakes.

The lockmaster radioed the pleasure boaters in the lock that upon exiting the lock they would see a dredge working in the river. He suggested that we should contact them on VHF channel 13 for directions. We followed his instructions and were told to wait for a barge to go through the broken dredge line and then go through, with caution. We followed his instructions and had no problem. Within a half mile we were at the entrance to the Cumberland River. Actually, the river's mouth was hidden behind a small island another quarter of a mile upstream. We entered the Cumberland and were surprised to find muddy water and swift current. The stream was not shallow but was narrow and contained some commercial activity: barges were moored along the edge and a few mussel fishermen were working the center channel upstream. We traveled up the Cumberland about 30.5 miles to the Barkley Dam and after a short wait we locked through. The rise at this lock was 47 feet according to calculations made from readings of the depth finder.

When the gates opened the view of Barkley Lake was beautiful. Where there had been very little boat traffic on the Cumberland River, there was now many boats of all descriptions and sizes on the water in front of us. We quickly located the channel markers to Green Turtle Bay Marina and soon tied up at the fuel dock to top off our fuel tanks. We were assigned slips; we actually shared one fifty foot slip, tied stern to stern.

We saw many boats, houseboats and luxury yachts in their slips and on the water. This is truly a marina to remember. The facilities are good to excellent, access to the lake is very easy and the dam is only a mile or less away. Showers, laundry, bathrooms and ships store are all nearby.

# July 24, 1994 Sunday

Green Turtle Bay Marina
Barkley Lake Mile, 32R
to
Duncan Bay Anchorage, Kentucky Lake
Tennessee River, Mile 34L

I changed the engine oil at the marina. There were 81 hours registered on the engine 'hour meter'. Jan and Doc rose early and got an early start on their laundry chores. Saundra slept late and did laundry later. This is a rest and resupply day so we have great difficulty in getting in any kind of hurry today. Doc and I had a nice walk trying to find a ships store that would sell oil and oil filters. We finally located a Bayliner dealer who sold oil. I told him of my problem with the distributor shaft housing and he said I might have a chance to get the manufacturer to replace the unit free of charge.

We left Green Turtle Bay Marina after lunch, about 2:30 p.m., and navigated the Barkley Canal to Kentucky Lake, then to Kentucky Lake Sails Marina. We tied to their fuel dock temporarily and shopped in their ships store. Saundra purchased a boat hook to replace a broken one I keep trying to repair. The dockmaster allowed us to have a temporary slip and we walked about a quarter mile to Patti's Restaurant.

We strolled through the grounds, gift shops and poked

35

our noses into the restaurants. They had caged animals on display but most of them were too smart to stay in the hot sun so we couldn't see them. They were hiding in their-cages out of the sun and out of sight. There were flowers, running water from a working fountain, shops and shady porches with benches to rest on. The heat was very oppressive and we took advantage of the opportunity to rest often. Saundra and Jan went to the Dairy Queen for Blizzards and Lemonade. We played tourist as we sipped our drinks and walked along the highway back to our boats.

We shoved off and cruised up Kentucky Lake for about twenty minutes to mile thirty-four Right and beached the *Saundra Kay* on a gravel bar in Duncan Bay, just inside and to the right. The cove on the opposite side of the gravel bar went unnoticed until we were secured and Roamer arrived and tied alongside.

We refreshed ourselves with drink and swam in the warm water. At about 8:30 p.m. dinner was being prepared over a fire on the gravel bar with Doc and I roasting hot dogs and kielbasa.

It was a great success! Steve was in charge of the indoor, on-board cooking where he prepared beans with potatoes and cucumber salad. We made pigs of ourselves again; at least I did.

The evening became quiet and as the lake water became still, the moon rose above the trees and cloud line. It painted a golden ribbon across the still water to our boats and we drank in the stillness of the night and the beauty of nature around us. Katydids serenaded us from the shores.

We retired to our bunks and slept fitfully because of the heat. Saundra found a different bunk during the night in an attempt to find cooler lodgings.

During the night Jan developed an uncomfortable reaction to the smoke from the smoldering campfire on shore. Our boat rocked as Doc walked our gunwales to get to shore where he doused the coals of our fire, hoping to eliminate the smoke and ease her discomfort.

# July 25, 1994 Monday

Duncan Bay Anchorage, Kentucky Lake
Tennessee River Mile 34R
to
Kelly's Island Anchorage
Tennessee River Mile 143L

However, upon awakening we learned the campfire on shore, although not smoking now, had caused an allergic reaction in Jan. She had developed the problem during the night and took medication to relieve breathing difficulties. Doc is still very concerned about giving Jan her next scheduled allergy shot. He said that it must be given when near a medical facility in case there is an adverse reaction. Our plan is to continue the cruise to the next facility near water where such service could be obtained in an emergency. Pickwick Landing looks like the best bet.

The boats were made ready and we shoved off at 8:05 a.m. Kentucky Lake was calm with small ripples from the morning breeze. We made good time until some cavitation of *Roamer's* propeller caused Doc to be concerned. It was only an occasional problem, usually when rough water from barge wakes or strong currents were encountered.

We stopped for fuel at Birdsong Marina after a grueling fifteen miles of beating into a very strong headwind. We met the owner/operator and learned he was running for county commissioner. On the way out of the marina I decided to take a shortcut through a narrow pass to the channel on the other side. I watched the depth finder closely as we approached. I raised the out drive as high as it would go but - too late! The *Saundra Kay* still ran aground on a mud bottom at a very slow speed. The depth meter showed one foot depth and a cloud of reflections glittered on the screen. I learned that the *Saundra Kay* could remove herself from mud in shallow water and against a strong wind from the stern. We backed off the mud and I left a wiser and better boater. We soon overtook *Roamer* and continued up the Tennessee River.

A bald eagle winged his way over the river and to say that he was majestic is an understatement. He was magnificent!

We arrived at Kelly's Island and pushed *Saundra Kay*'s bow into a high sand bank at 4:30 p.m. A strong current made it necessary to tie a line to a tree upstream at a forty-five degree angle. A bow line was secured dead ahead to a tree, and *Roamer* tied alongside us with her line downstream to another tree.

We swam and Doc checked his propeller, pronounced it okay, and we enjoyed refreshing drinks and Jan's snack tray (a nightly treat.) The rain that had threatened all day seemed far away now, but our ace weather man Steve 'Old thunder and lightning' Grant, is certain we will get rain tonight.

Dinner was served at the fashionable hour of 7:30 p.m. I smoked the ham and Saundra announced that it was a seven course dinner served in cans and plastic bags. It looked like the cooks didn't want to do dishes tonight!

Before settling down for the night *Saundra Kay*'s bow had to be pushed away from the sand bank in order to make the V berth level for sleeping. The lines were loosened at the bow and at the stern cleat. I positioned myself under the bow with my back firmly situated to lift and push the boat backward. With Doc and Steve in position, Jan and Saundra stood in the rear of the boat to take weight off the bow. I lifted mightily and the boat moved slightly; again, and gained more. Then on the third push the boat lurched backward and I lost my footing in the shifting sand. Into the water I went with a loud splash! I rose quickly with the aid of the bow line and promptly repeated the act! Doc and Steve howled with laughter as I struggled to remove myself from the sandy muck. We finally retired for the night.

Our anchorage behind Kelly's Island was a secure place to spend the evening and night. A heavy rain fell during the night, as Steve had predicted, and washed some of the sand bank into the channel. A large tow descended the river and cast his searchlight into our area and awakened some of the sleeping crew.

## July 26, 1994 Tuesday

Kelly's Island Anchorage
Tennessee River Mile 143L
to
Pickwick Park Landing and Dock
Tennessee River Mile 207.6L

In the morning all was wet around us. Saundra sat in the cabin with a glaze over her eyes after a night of interrupted sleep, heat, mosquito bites, thunder storms, and listening to the sound of sand beside the boat slipping slowly into the water. I had seen that look before: usually in the eyes of depraved killers in horror movies or newspaper mug shots of convicted criminals. She is not happy. It will be my job to change her mood today. My plan is to find a shower for her somewhere and ply her with ice cream. Doc and Jan are rather quiet today, anxious to get to the Pickwick Lake area so Jan can get her allergy shot.

The morning was clear and sunny with shade from the trees along the island casting a cooling umbrella over our beached craft. Doc is still concerned about the noisy outdrive unit which periodically caused him to decrease speed to stop the grinding noise coming from the defective unit. At about 7:30 a.m., they cast off and headed upstream to test the engine and outdrive and get a head start toward Pickwick Lake for repairs at Aqua Marine Yacht Club - a Volvo-Penta repair facility.

By 8:10 a.m. the *Saundra Kay* was under way and making the turn out of the channel and into the Tennessee River. We sighted the *Roamer* immediately making her way downstream. Doc called on the radio and explained that he wanted to go eight miles back down the river to a marina where he could get a mechanic to change his propeller. As they started on downstream we pulled out into the river and spotted the *Molly B* of Heartland Boating magazine fame, headed upstream. We hailed her on radio and exchanged greetings.

The *Saundra Kay* escorted the crippled *Roamer* to Michael's Marina in Perryville and tied up. Doc found a mechanic to change the propeller. The mechanic asked the three men to sit on Roamers bow and said he needed a "couple fat ladies." Saundra and Jan ignored his comment.

Doc took *Roamer* out to test the new propeller but came right back in as that was not the problem. The staff at Michael's Perrysville Marina were very helpful and concerned about our situation but they were unequipped to work on Volvo engines or outdrives. Doc made phone calls to other Marinas. Birdsong Marina or Aqua Harbor Yacht Club were the choices. Doc asked Aqua Harbor if they had a trailer to come get *Roamer*. The reply was to try to get the craft upstream ... **eighty-two more miles**!

Checking the *Roamer*'s propeller

Doc gave Jan her allergy shot while waiting for the phone calls and no major problems occurred.

Doc decided to make a run for the facility at Pickwick Lake so we cast off at 11:15 a.m. Since they were limited in speed we decided to leap-frog our way to Pickwick. That is to say that *Roamer* would run ahead for approximately four miles, then *Saundra Kay* would run on plane, overtake *Roamer* and continue until radio contact became garbled at twenty-five watt power, then beach and wait for *Roamer* to catch up. This was repeated until we reached mile 171.8L at Saltillo and Scotties Marina. A narrow channel entrance and a sharp turn to port and we were in a shallow lagoon.

We refueled, (slightly pricey) and viewed the

cottonmouth moccasin skin on the wall as well as the picture of the snake before it met its fate. The photo was marked "23 Lbs." which Scottie said was the original weight of the snake. A collection of American Indian arrowheads was displayed on the walls and Scottie explained that some were from nearby burial grounds. He handed Saundra a gosling still in the downy stage which she held and petted. Scottie assured her that it only *poops* once a day. We were skeptical and I noticed that Saundra kept a wary eye on the chick and Scottie.

Scottie asked whether anyone would be interested in buying a larger boat, mentioning that the large wooden Chris Craft might be traded for my boat. I declined after he said it would need about one year's work to repair her. We did not linger at Scottie's but continued to *leapfrog* up the Tennessee River.

*Roamer* was causing Doc to doubt her ability to make our destination by nightfall. He suggested we beach behind Diamond Island at Tennessee River Mile 196 but I convinced him to continue the remaining 11 miles to the lock and Pickwick Lake. This would give us an overnight slip with light and electricity, water and showers etc. He agreed and we continued upriver.

The *Saundra Kay* arrived at the lock at 5:51 p.m. and contacted the lockmaster. He said he was preparing the lock for the houseboat waiting at the entrance and instructed me to go into the lock behind him. We explained *Roamer's* situation and the lockmaster said we could wait for *Roamer* if she wasn't too long in arriving. We contacted Doc and found they were about five miles behind us. Doc was very concerned that we not leave through the lock without them.

We waited ten minutes and contacted *Roamer* again to

check his speed and ETA. According to Doc's estimated position he was making a mile every five minutes. At that rate he would need fifteen to twenty minutes to reach the lock. We told the lockmaster that we didn't want to delay the houseboat but also did not want to leave our companions behind in case they needed help. The lockmaster understood but reminded us that if a barge approached we would lose our turn. About the time that conversation ended and we had tied to the wall outside the lock, *Roamer* rounded the bend into view. We contacted the lockmaster who informed us that he had the boat in view. He agreed for us to lock through with the house boat, told us all to wear life jackets, position our boat at the 200 foot mark with the bumpers on our starboard side. *Roamer* came into the lock and tied at the 400 foot mark, the gates closed and we soon locked through the 55 foot lift into Pickwick Lake. We arrived at Pickwick Landing State Park Docks at 6:58 p.m.

We refueled and tied up for the night. Our rates were: Gas - $1.35 per gallon, slip with 30 Amp service, & potable water = $00.40 per foot of boat length.

Steve, after piloting and navigating all day, volunteered to cook his now famous tuna noodle casserole. Doc and I prepared many carrot sticks to munch with dinner. Jan added her homemade bread and Saundra handed out the butter and we were eating a delicious dinner. A very strong thunder storm sweeping through the area had skirted us but now drenched us with steady rain during our meal.

Rain continued into the night and cooled the air for a great night of sleep.

## July 27, 1994 Wednesday

Pickwick Park Landing and Dock
Tennessee River Mile 207.6L
to
Aqua Marine Harbor, Tenn-Tom Mile 448.5L

We slept late, till about eight o'clock under overcast skies. Everything is wet but swept clean by the overnight rain. *Roamer's* troubles have kept Doc and Jan in an uneasy state of mind for the past two days. They shoved off for the repair facility at 8:20 a.m. this morning. We stayed behind to rest and recuperate, use the shower facility and generally gather ourselves for the next leg of the cruise. We are not sure at this point whether we will be going the rest of the way alone or with Doc and Jan. It appears to depend on the recommendation of the Aqua Marine Harbor mechanics. In either case, with or without our friends, we must continue to our destination. The *Saundra Kay*, a sturdy boat with a strong engine and a determined crew, will not be stopped.

After cleaning our boat and having a light lunch we shoved off to rendezvous with *Roamer* at the entrance to the Tenn-Tom Waterway on Yellow Creek. We arrived at about 2:30 p.m. and met Doc and Jan at the transient pier. They are waiting to move their boat to a slip assigned to hold them until *Roamer* can be hauled out and the engine and outdrive evaluated. This process is expected to take two days. Doc informed us that this is the end of the cruise for them, and remarked "Even Lee had to give up sometime."

Doc and Jan plan to stay until the evaluation is completed then return home by rental car. Jan said that at least they had gotten us to within three hundred and fifty miles of our destination. Doc reminded us that we had been in three states today; Alabama, Mississippi and Tennessee.

We shared a champagne toast to the completion of the first 1,235 miles of the cruise. I suggested that we share a last dinner aboard the *Saundra Kay* before we continue *our* cruise up the beautiful Tennessee River. Steve, Saundra and I plan to spend the evening and night at Cooper Hollow waterfall which is only a few miles from our present location. Hopefully we can rest there and review our plans and schedule for the remaining three hundred and fifty mile cruise. Saundra is intent on arriving per our original schedule. That is, Saturday afternoon, July 30, 1994. I assure her that it will not be a problem unless we encounter more mechanical troubles.

Jan brought a delicious tray of snacks while a dinner of tuna-macaroni salad was being prepared. After dinner we bid farewell to Doc and Jan and left for nearby Cooper Hollow waterfall.

It was seven in the evening. By seven forty-five we arrived at the waterfall and found three sailboats there, two riding at anchor and one beached on a sandbar just inside the narrow mouth of the cove to the right. The large sandbar blocking the right side of the mouth of the cove looks like the perfect place to beach our boat for a view of the waterfall over the stern. But the sailboat already occupied a place near the narrow end and we didn't want to intrude on their space. We idled into the cove, and were discussing our options for anchorage for the night when we were hailed by a lady from the sailboat on the sandbar. We told her we planned to stay here for the night and she invited us to beach beside her boat. We gladly accepted her invitation and beached our boat alongside and tied the bow and port stern cleat securely to small trees on the shore.

This waterfall, though not spectacular, is worthy of the efforts of a landscape artist. It is a rock face about seventy-five feet across at the base and is stair-stepped to about forty feet in height. Water cascades down the entire face of the formation with the largest flow coming down the right side. A constant sound of falling water echoes across the cove to its mouth some three hundred yards distant to the east. A slow, westerly breeze blew from the falls to the mouth of the cove carrying a slight mist about three feet above the surface of the water.

Saundra and Bill enjoy Cooper Hollow Waterfall

At eight o'clock a small outboard motorboat arrived at the falls carrying three young men. They tied up at the base of the falls and swam and dived from the face of the falls for about an hour. They left, and the evening and night are beautiful and peaceful. The katydids, crickets and the falls lulled us to sleep.

I awoke during the night to see a half moon directly overhead through the hatch. The light had disturbed my slumber so I went to the stern of the boat to see the effect of the moonlight on the waterfall. The scene was spectacular! With the falls beyond a blanket of dense fog over the water it looked like a layer of puffy, white clouds in the moon's light. No water was visible under the fog. It appeared as though the water from the falls just disappeared into the white foam. It was a sight I'm glad I didn't miss.

# July 28, 1994 Thursday

Cooper Hollow Waterfall, Pickwick Lake
Tennessee River, Mile 217.2L
to
Limestone Creek anchorage, Wheeler Lake
Tennessee River, Mile 310.8R

At six thirty this morning a chill crept over the boat from the fog laden breeze off the waterfall. The boat seemed to be riding high in the bow and low in the stern and was not floating free in the water as it was the night before. I went forward on the deck and discovered, to my amazement, that we were firmly aground on the beach. The lake level appeared to have dropped two feet overnight. The twenty-seven foot sailboat beached alongside us appeared to rise dramatically higher at her bow and seemed to be resting firmly on her keel. We decided to enjoy our coffee before we attempted to tackle the problem.

Brother and sister, Steve Grant and Saundra Gillum
Enjoying the morning in Cooper Hollow

Steve agreed that we could push off from the sandbar unless the water dropped more. He and I would loosen the lines and push our boat off the sandbar with our backs.

Steve and I snugged up against the underside of the bow, and on multiple counts of one-two-three-heave! We finally inched the *Saundra Kay* backwards, until she floated free.

Elated at our success, we studied the thirty-two foot sailboat resting in her sandy bed and wondered whether we should wake the sleeping crew and advise them of their situation, or be polite and wait for them to discover their plight. Suddenly the sailboat heeled over toward the *Saundra Kay*; her tall mast coming to rest above our boat. A loud thud came from within the sailboat followed by excited voices and peals of laughter. A female face peered from the cockpit and excitedly explained that she had gone to the head and the shift in weight had tipped the boat. Her friend had then fallen from her bunk onto the deck below.

After much laughter and discussion, a joint attempt to push the sailboat off the sand failed. Then the *Saundra Kay* took the sailboat in tow, tied stern to stern. The third attempt under power was successful and the sailboat floated free and level. We left the Cooper Hollow waterfall at 8:11 a.m.

The weather was very pleasant with puffy white clouds in a blue sky. The temperature was in the low eighties. Water conditions were good with a slight chop in some stretches of the lake. We cruised to Wilson Lock and Dam at Tennessee River Mile 259.5. The approach to this lock is via a channel about three and a half miles long. Just below the entrance to the canal the Mississippi Queen stern-wheeler was offloading passengers on the shore. She was firing her boilers as we passed her. We slowed to admire her then continued to the lock. We were not allowed to enter the lock until the Yazoo City barge locked through, a two hour wait. We tied to the lock wall, had lunch, and waited while a TVA barge also locked through ahead of us. About two and a half hours was spent waiting. Finally, the lockmaster let us through at two thirty in the afternoon. This lock was very impressive with a lift of ninety-three feet.

Once Wilson Lock and Dam was finally behind us we sped toward Wheeler Dam at 'warp speed', but if the Yazoo City tow arrives at the locks before us, we could have another two and a half hour wait for her to lock through. Instead, we found a quiet spot and anchored for an hour and a half, then cruised to the arrival point below the dam.

The motor yacht *Betty Sue* was also waiting, tied to the lock wall. Her skipper volunteered to walk over to us on the wall and tied us off on a stationary bitt. While we waited for the Yazoo City to lock through again, we saw the ten foot high plume of discharge water from the lock chamber as it emptied. Wheeler lock has a lift of forty eight feet and the escaping water rising with such force is very impressive.

Steve Grant, as the Wheeler Lock exhausts a plume of water

Our total time waiting and locking through was four hours. We were on our way again by six thirty in the evening. We were not making up any time on our schedule and we hoped to pick up a few miles by now. These two lock delays were the first since leaving Greene Cove, an amazing stroke of luck!

At Lucy's Branch Marina we stopped for fuel but discovered they had already *read* their pumps. I asked them to reopen their pumps and they graciously complied. It is a very nice stop, and convenient to the lake. About a mile away Saundra noticed that she had left her phone book at the marina and we had to return to retrieve the runaway book. This cost precious time and as night began to fall, Steve and I scanned the charts for a logical anchorage for the night. Limestone Creek was our choice. We knew that it would mean some running in the dark, but Saundra, who fears running at night, was game, so we went ahead with the plan. Steve watched the charts and I made the one million candle power spotlight ready on the bridge. As we approached Decatur, Alabama dark was upon us and we were running from buoy - to can buoy - to marker - to landmark in the dark, with the aid of the searchlight.

Bass boats surged around us, some without running lights burning. One came head on, barely visible in the gloom, spray flying in a seventy mile per hour arc off the stern. I held my course and gave a warning blast on my horn and he swerved to starboard then zoomed past on my port side.

Decatur is a magnificent city fully lighted against the night sky. This is a beautiful scene if you are star struck lovers on a nightly walk. For serious boaters, bent on making time over the water without losing life, limb or property, it is not so beautiful. Steve held firm, studying the charts to locate the channel marker buoys and illuminating them, one by one, as we cruised through the night. We maintained good speed and soon neared the far side of Decatur where we were stopped by a railroad bridge too low for us to pass under. Bass boats were able to buzz beneath the bridge. We didn't know whether to find a place to tie up until dawn or to try calling on channel 16 for help. Steve hailed the bridge operator on channel 16 and he replied after a train passed over the bridge. The lift bridge operator said he could raise the bridge as soon as the train was the proper distance away. He asked the size of our boat and wanted to know how much height we would need. Steve gave him the information and he said he would raise the bridge to forty feet. The bridge raised, the green light went on, and we passed under the span.

A tall bridge was ahead of us and suddenly a very bright spotlight illuminated us from beneath the bridge. I didn't know what was going on so we continued cautiously and slowly passed under the bridge. Then we could see construction, dredging and such bridge building activity was being conducted. The spot light was from a work barge without front lights. We proceeded at idle speed around the barge and the work area into an unmarked channel. Using our spot light, Steve located the shore line and we went up the channel, around and between bass boats, toward our anchorage in Limestone Creek.

The dual span bridge of Route 65, which we noted on our charts, lay ahead; about a mile and a tenth beyond was the mouth of Limestone Creek. The creek was hard to locate because of the large growth of brush and tree limbs at its mouth. The *Saundra Kay* idled up the creek for about two hundred yards before we dropped bow and stern anchors at nine-thirty. Saundra quickly prepared dinner while Steve and I made sure everything was buttoned up against the hordes of mosquitoes and insects trying to get into our lighted cabin. Soon after dinner, the crew turned in for the night, tired but pleased with our efforts and successes today.

# July 29, 1994 Friday

Limestone Creek Anchorage
Tennessee River, Mile 310.8R
to
Chickamauga Lake Anchorage
Tennessee River, Mile 475.8L

This morning was slightly foggy but the mist lay close to the water's surface. Chances were good for a clear, crisp day and for good cruising. Hopefully we have seen the last of the Yazoo City barge and with some of our old luck in locking through we could really make up some time today. We weighed anchor and headed upriver at 6:37 a.m. There is little activity on the smooth water and no traffic except for an occasional fisherman. It's too early for the Friday crowd!

Our progress is good up the river channel and as we near the Guntersville Lock and Dam the scenery is breathtaking! Mirror smooth pools of water reflect limestone rock outcroppings along the shore. We met a whitetail deer in midstream, crossing between Morgan and Madison Counties in Alabama. As we headed toward the towering rock formation in the bend of the river we saw our old nemesis, the Yazoo City, closely followed by another heavy tow. The following tow was passed in the bend but the Yazoo City blocked the channel with her bulk until we neared the locks. I ran to her starboard side and passed her. I couldn't believe our luck when Steve radioed the lockmaster at Guntersville Lock and was instructed to enter the auxiliary chamber for immediate lockage!

Once on Guntersville Lake we headed for Guntersville Marina for fuel and to go to town for supplies. Saundra decided to stay with the boat and clean the cabin while Steve and I walked the four blocks into town for groceries. It was a very pleasant town. We met a constable on his mid-morning rounds, nightstick in hand, a friendly smile and a warm greeting. Soon we were back aboard and underway again. As we left the Marina to our delight we saw the Yazoo City barge heading toward a *fleeting location* or terminal nearby.

The scenery soon changed to a more mountainous terrain with outcroppings of rock easily visible from the river.

At 11:42 a.m., we dropped anchor in a cove near Tennessee River Mile 379R and enjoyed lunch. Soon we crossed from Alabama into Tennessee and arrived at Nickajack Lock and Dam at 2:56 p.m. This lock with a 39 foot lift leads to the most scenic stretch of the Tennessee River with towering mountain vistas around every bend for miles.

As we passed by Chattanooga we saw two sternwheelers, including the beautiful *Southern Belle* in front of the city's impressive downtown waterfront.

The current was running swift just above Chattanooga, so we went to the area behind McClelland's Island to anchor for the night. The current was too swift there too, so we felt it wasn't a good spot to anchor. There were houses on the bluff high above us and we didn't have the privacy that we had become accustomed to. We decided to look for better anchorage with the full agreement of our First Mate.

Strong current is encountered as we approach the Chickamauga Lock and Dam. The reason is soon apparent; water is being released over the dam and a very rough chop is present directly in front of the lock entry point and downstream. The lockmaster said he was preparing the lock and we approached with caution. In an effort to stabilize our boat I idled toward the lock wall, hoping to find calmer water. A high chop of approximately two feet is present within and between the lock walls. Suddenly the lockmaster's voice could be heard telling us that the pleasure craft should not proceed further into the lock but hold her position. This was not good news. We were bouncing mightily on the choppy water and I feared that the side of the boat would be dashed against the walls. I instructed Saundra and Steve to be steady and not move about but hold their positions. I tied a large bumper on the port side forward and asked Saundra to tie a large bumper on the port side stern. She did. The boat never struck the wall but just rose and fell with the waves inside the enclosure. The lock gates swung open and we were instructed to enter and tie to a bitt. Once inside, the 48 foot lift went smoothly.

Just above the locks in Chickamauga Lake at Tennessee River mile 475.8R we dropped anchor in a cove. Steve swam in the cool water. The propane grill was lit and hamburgers were prepared for grilling. Since neither Steve nor I were familiar with the new grill we may have set the temperature too high. Anyway, during our frantic efforts to turn the burning burgers before they became blackened, a burger managed to fall from the grill and splat onto the swim platform below. We decided that this was a viable test of a hamburger's readiness to be eaten. The food was great, again!

After dinner, the threatening sky changed and a storm front veered around us. Everyone had a restful night in the cove.

# July 30, 1994 Saturday

Chickamauga Lake
Tennessee River Anchorage, Mile 475.8R
to
Watts Bar Lake, Pin Oak Pointe Home Port
Tennessee River, Mile 559.6R

Today is expected to be an easy day of cruising with only one lock, Watts Bar, and eighty-six miles to cover till we reach our final destination - the site of our future home. Our one concern was the Coast Guard radio security alert that Watts Bar Lock was closed until further notice. The reason for the closure was for scheduled repairs and according to the report they were encountering problems with the upstream lock gate. Our crew decided to continue and expect the Corps of Engineers to have done their work by the time we arrive at the lock.

When we reached the arrival point below the lock, Steve radioed the lockmaster and was told that the lock was in operation. He instructed us to approach the lock and he would reopen the gates which he'd just closed prior to receiving our call. We were to *raft off* to the pleasure craft already inside, which happened to be approximately our size. We entered slowly and idled to the far starboard side of the lock. The crew aboard the *Family Affair*, a Sea Ray, was preparing to raft to us. As we tied off to them Saundra said, "That's Randy Jones!" Sure enough, this was the gentleman we had met at Harbor Point Marina in the early spring when we had last visited the lake and investigated some of the area Marinas. We had talked to Randy and his assistant, Gerald, at length at that time and had enjoyed our visit very much. He was on a trip with the new owner of *Family Affair*, a very nice gentleman who is a school principal, to familiarize him with its operation. The new owner was obviously delighted with his first boat. We wished him well and good boating.

The fifty-eight foot vertical lift was slow because the lock was able to use only one pump. It may have been best, since we were rafted off to another boat and didn't need another challenge in a lock at this time.

Our instructions were to exit the lock slowly since divers were down and the *No Wake* requirement was a must. We complied, of course.

The first impression of our home pool, Watts Bar Lake, was very favorable.

She is clear and wide and a nice blue color. Any doubts I had about our selection of this location evaporated with the first view. Small ridges rise beyond the shores and some rock outcroppings can be seen occasionally. Fishing is obviously good as evidenced by the many bass boats we saw along the way.

We cruised alongside the *Family Affair* for several miles until they changed course to take advantage of a small craft pass which cuts off several miles from the main channel. We pulled in behind them at Harbor Point Marina, topped off our fuel tank, purchased ice and used the facilities. As we left, Randy offered to provide a covered slip, with all services on a weekly or monthly basis to help us get through the summer. With thanks to Randy we were soon on our way to our own dock at Tennessee Mile 559.6R. We arrived at two-thirty in the afternoon on July 30, 1994, exactly on schedule and then decided to idle up the shoreline and view the area from the water for the first time. We said hello to some neighbors who were on their docks and told them of our plans to stay and build a home. They seemed anxious to have more neighbors at Pin Oak Pointe and welcomed us to Tennessee. We idled back to our dock and met Dick Clayton, the builder. Dick helped us tie up; it was good to see him again.

The hickory tree which shaded part of the dock had grown a limb that came near our bow rail when we were tied up. I managed to remove the limb but another, larger limb was too much for my hacksaw, and the blade broke.

Large numbers of mayflies were hanging from the tree limbs and we wondered if we would be in trouble tonight. I went up the steep bank of our lot to a 1986 Fierro which had been parked behind a locust bush thicket for the last month. The engine started on the first try. We have wheels!

We all inspected the lot we had purchased months earlier. Covered with trees, bushes and vines of all descriptions (some good, some not so good), it could definitely be described as 'unimproved'. We recognized that we would have a lot of work ahead of us to prepare this lot for a house, to build a house and establish a new home. We were excited about the prospect and the challenge of living on our small boat during the entire process. I showed Steve the property boundary lines. He liked the location and the lake as well and expressed his approval of the dock design.

Our eldest son, James, and our daughter-in-law, Paulette, were to meet us this afternoon if we were on schedule. As the evening wore on I began to think they were going to wait until tomorrow to bring our other car over from Greeneville, South Carolina. To my surprise they came bounding through the woods at about the same time the mayflies started swarming all over the boat and dock. Chewey, their golden retriever, was with them and he bounded happily down the steps and onto the dock.

To our amazement the mayflies quickly covered the boat and light post and in a short time I was looking at a one inch thick mass of flies along the gunwale of the *Saundra Kay*. Fish were in a feeding frenzy as the hapless flies fell into the water. I scraped flies up with a dustpan and dumped them into the swirling water. The small fish feeding on the flies were apparently attracting larger predator fish as indicated by the large swirls and splashes which could be seen and heard in the darkness. Chewey snapped and pawed at the flies, making a game of it.

James and Paulette pitched a tent at the edge of the woods above the boat and we were all soon tucked in for the night.

### July 31, 1994 Sunday

First full day at Pin Oak Pointe

Today we all slept until 7:30 a.m., then got ourselves together and went to the Cracker Barrel Restaurant in Harriman for a big breakfast. We returned and cleaned more flies off the boat, loaded everyone on board and headed up the lake to a nearby cove. Chewey delighted everyone by jumping in the water from the swim platform and swimming like golden retrievers are born to do. The water was refreshingly cool and we all enjoyed the swim. Saundra chose to stay aboard while Chewey played water Frisbee with James and Paulette and was a real *waterdog*.

Back on our dock we grilled hamburgers on the propane grill we had mounted on the dock rail. They were outstanding again!

After dinner our 'kids' left for South Carolina at about four o'clock.

Steve and I drove the Fierro to the Rockwood Airport to check on their facilities. Some gentlemen were sitting on the patio discussing life and we talked with them at length. One was a local builder working on a new house on lot 67 in Pin Oak Pointe. They were all interesting and we hated to leave for Rockwood to make the telephone call for Steve's pilot friend to fly him back to his home in Ohio. We made the call and returned to our dock by nine p.m.

Saundra and Steve soon headed to their beds and I stayed up trying to catch up on the ship's log. We had buttoned up the boat in an attempt to foil the mayflies but morning proved that they are still here as they covered the boat but in a more scattered way.

While I was typing on the Laptop computer about eleven p.m., I had the feeling that I was being watched. You know the one when the hair stands up on your neck and you assume a defensive attitude. Well, I turned around and looked out through the plastic covering the stern of the boat. Two men stood directly behind the boat, and appearing at first to be touching the boat they were so close. An eerie fluorescent light cast a strange bluish pallor over their expressionless faces. Ghostly looking were these two, slowly gliding past our boat without a sound and disappearing into the gloom. When the chill bumps had disappeared from my back and my neck hair had lain down, I realized they were not ghosts, only night fishermen after bass. I poured myself another Jim Beam over ice and typed on.

On Tuesday evening, Steve's friend arrived in a Piper Cub, and they left for Ohio from the Rockwood Airport.

We've enjoyed his company very much and hope he visits us often. Saundra and I are alone and ready, even anxious, to begin work on the lot. We plan to build a house and invite our friends to visit us here.

*Captain Bill Gillum*
*August 2, 1994*

# Afterword

"Cruise of the Rivers" was completed in its final version on January 22, 2001, over six years after the cruise ended. During this time we have seen many changes in our situation since arriving in Tennessee.

At first we made arrangements with a local barge operator to drive telephone poles for an extension of our boat dock. When the construction barge arrived and was driving the poles we anchored about two hundred feet away and I fished for bass with a spinning rod and plastic worm. I was pleasantly surprised to catch a largemouth bass of approximately three pounds while the pile driver was noisily in operation. This seemed an omen of great fishing to come. The barge operator asked me to stop catching fish since it was causing his crew to stop and watch.

Clearing our lot was a long and difficult chore. We needed tools to cut the bushes and small trees, so we went to Browder's Hardware in Kingston. There I met Bill, a salesman of the highest order. He sold me a crooked mattock, "the last one we have" and a crooked handle to fit it, also "the last one we have." I still have that ugly tool and won't part with it. The lot was bush-hogged where the growth was not too tall and the chopped up brush, weeds and grass left an ugly layer of drying rubble on the ground.

About that time Saundra and I were sitting in the boat doing nothing in particular when an inboard/outboard boat came around the shore and idled toward us. The driver of the boat hailed us and we exchanged greetings and small talk. He was very friendly and seemed curious about what we were up to. I invited him aboard and he pulled his craft alongside our swim platform and came into the canvas covered aft cockpit of the *Saundra Kay*. He said he was JD Robertson and was on his way to Lot number five in Pin Oak Pointe, the namesake lot of the development. He had bought the lot in the initial auction a couple of years ago and was planning to eventually build a log home on the site.

Occasionally he would run his boat from Kingston to check on his property.

JD seemed curious about our plans to clear the lot and stay on the boat while we build our home. He told me that he was here to do whatever I needed done. This seemed strange to me coming from a total stranger and I asked, "Mr. Robertson, just what is it that you plan to do for me?" He seemed strangely amused by this but replied, "Well, If you need a doctor or dentist I can recommend one, if you need information on local builders, electricians, plumbers, mechanics etc. I can help you there too." He seemed totally sincere and Saundra and I felt we had found a real friend. He was as good as his word and more. He helped us through a hot summer of clearing the lot and fighting boredom on the boat by hosting us to delicious dinners at his log home near Kingston. His lovely wife, Ann was a great cook and a real worker.

JD and Ann helped us clear the briars and bushes from the lot, pile and burn them in the hot August sun. During an especially hot afternoon in August, Ann and I were raking and piling brush when Ann told me to get in some shade and cool off. She just kept on working. JD was riding his lawnmower over the high stubble, knocking it down in a cloud of dust. He looked at me and grinned. "She can't help it," he said, "She's from Alabama and just loves to work." Though they never built the log home on lot five due to health concerns, they are living in Kingston in their condominium about eight miles away. Their many acts of kindness and generosity to us will never be forgotten.

Late fall is when the lake level drops for the winter months.

By the end of November the lake is resting at winter

pool level, five feet lower than in the summer. This meant that our boat would float below the dock level. The flying bridge will be at the same level as the dock so we'll exit the cabin, ascend the stepladder to the flying bridge, go across it and step to the edge of the dock. A misstep here and you could fall about ten feet into the shallow water between the boat and the pilings. Once on the edge of the dock, we had to hold a safety rope and walk a plank across eight feet of open space to the finished part of the dock. This would be our arrangement until spring, when the dock builder finished the decking on the added section of dock.

During the fall and winter when I wasn't otherwise occupied, I busied myself carrying rocks in a wheelbarrow from the lot to the edge of the dry lake shoreline.

I used these rocks to riprap the shoreline that fronted our property for approximately fifty feet. This section had some severely undercut banks and in order to stabilize the area I had to fill the cavities with stone. I placed about seventy-five ton of stone along this shoreline by hand. At some points it was ten feet thick at the base due to the undercuts. My weight shifted and my waistline showed it. It probably was the best thing for my health.

By January 29, 1995 we were able to begin construction of our lake home.

It is a small place, 1,200 square feet designed to face the lake with an all glass wall of sliding doors and matching glass panels arranged in a letter "C" shape. A wooden deck faces the lake. A large activity room is in the center with a bedroom and bath on both ends. A stone fireplace is in the center of the activity room wall opposite the lake. It has a great view of the lake and we feel it is perfect for a retirement home. By March we were able to move in, and none too soon. We had been on the boat a very long time and were glad to have some space. Again, neighbors came to our aid with the loan of an air mattress to use until we could get our furniture out of storage. We painted the house inside and out and were involved in the actual construction in small ways. Now we were really "at home."

In the years since moving into our home we have come to know many interesting and wonderful people. Our little neighborhood has grown from two houses to seventeen, we have a neighborhood organization, a stone entrance sign and are currently building our own city water system. Saundra and I have found interesting part-time employment at the local Potter's Ace Hardware store in Harriman. Last year we extended the original deck by 632 square feet and added a hot tub and sauna.

All is not rosy however as Saundra and I have both incurred some health problems. Two years ago I had to have triple bypass surgery due to clogged arteries and Saundra had to have a stent placed in a restricted artery. I guess our inherited problems and our unhealthy lifestyles of the past have come home to roost. But we both agree that our little place in Tennessee is the place we want to call home. We will probably not work much longer so we can spend more time doing the things people really retire to do. Next year, we hope to take the *Saundra Kay* down the Tennessee River and Tenn-Tom Waterway to the gulf. But that will be another story.

# Interlude

## Time to plan for the next trip

The cold rain slowly penetrated my insulated shirt and began to ooze down the middle of my back toward my lower parts. Every movement made the fabric stick to my skin and the sharp feeling of a cool, wet shirt suddenly against my back sent a shock through me. I desperately hoped the rain would stop or slack off, or that Spencer would decide he couldn't stand it any longer and take my suggestion to quit and come back tomorrow. But oh no, he just kept sawing the dead pines into manageable sized pieces and I doggedly kept dragging them to a pile. This is December 7th, 2001 and we are cutting dead pine trees to earn money to pay for a boat trip next year. We are pooling our earnings, less expenses, with the hope that we will be able to earn enough for a month-long trip on the Tennessee River and perhaps the Tenn-Tom Waterway to Mobile Bay.

Spencer Whalen is sixty-two years old (nearly sixty-three), six foot two with dark hair thinning on top, and a black mustache. He carries his 200 pounds easily on a well-muscled, athletic frame. His arms are well muscled and as you can imagine he tends to charm the ladies with his quiet demeanor and infrequent smile. Born on the border of Roane and Morgan Counties near Harriman, Tennessee, Spencer is one of the many native sons who migrated north to the industrial cities for work in their factories. Dayton, Ohio, was Spencer's home for most of his working life. He eventually tired of the tire building business and returned to his 'home place' where he had built a house on fifteen acres of hillside wooded land. A steep, half-mile gravel road leads to his secluded home.

Carolyn, his wife of nearly three years, is the opposite. She is a southern born lady with a twinkle in her eye, a ready smile, and infectious laugh. She is tall with dark hair and creamy skin that tans easily. Carolyn is about five years Spencer's junior. We consider Carolyn and Spencer to be our very special friends.

Saundra, my wife of nearly forty-one years, and I are just the opposite of our friends. At five-five and five-eight respectively, we are by today's averages, considered short. We have light skin color and both were red-haired when we were young. Saundra still has natural red hair but my hair is totally white. I am sixty-three and Saundra is fifty-nine years old. I have been retired from Lucent Technologies since 1994. We relocated from Pittsburgh, PA to Rockwood, TN on Watts Bar Lake on the Tennessee River, Mile 559.6R.

Our boat, the *Saundra Kay*, a 25 foot Bayliner cabin cruiser, was run to Blue Springs Marina on December first to have her rub rail repaired, bottom cleaned, painted, and have the engine tuned as well as other maintenance performed on the out-drive. This is all being done in preparation for our boat trip down the river next summer. This boat sleeps six but that is really pushing it on a long trip. We believe four passengers will be the maximum number for comfort and compatibility.

Hoping to make some extra spending money, Spencer took a weekend job to trim a few limbs from a shade tree in front of a lady's home. He volunteered to do it not knowing if the lady intended to pay him. He invited me to join him and away we went, loaded with chain saws, rakes, ropes and any tool we thought the job might take. Before we were through with the limb removal job, we found ourselves contracted to cut dead pine trees and stack them on a small hill behind her house.

One thing led to another and before we knew it we had priced jobs to cut and remove trees from two of her neighbors' properties as well. The initial customer insisted that she *must* pay us so we gladly accepted. After all, this was extremely physical work and by the end of an eight-hour day we looked really dirty, were soaked with sweat, and totally exhausted.

Spencer suggested we put our first check in a savings account to spend on a summer boating trip down the Tennessee River. I agreed and we were off to the races, or more correctly, to the woods.

We estimated that we would require four thousand dollars to cover expenses for a four-week round trip down the river system, no matter what destination we chose. So we made that our objective. (More would be better.) So far, we are doing well. In only four weekends we are almost halfway to our goal. Remember, we are in our sixties and not really accustomed to hard physical labor.

Spencer told me, after an especially hard day of cutting and stacking trees in a slow, drizzling rain, he was exhausted. He was so tired, in fact, that shortly after arriving home, he'd just settled into a comfortable recliner when he heard a noise at his front door. He opened the door and was amazed to see his own ass standing there! I told him that maybe we had better quit a little earlier the next day we worked. It probably doesn't help that he is working a four day, forty hour week for a local hardware store as a salesman at its contractor sales desk.

## December 18, 2001

Today, Tuesday, December 18, 2001, I received a telephone call from Carey Bishop, a local mechanic who specializes in repairs and service to boats in this area. He reported that he had completed changing the distributor cap and rotor, sacrificial anodes and spark plug wires on the *Saundra Kay*. A new bilge pump had been installed in the engine compartment and the out drive inspected and serviced, water in the block had been drained, and the engine was winterized. In his opinion, new paint was not needed on the out drive unit at this time. The engine had been tested out of the water by using a water hose and it was discovered that the automatic choke was not opening at all after the engine warmed up. That explained to me why the engine had seemed to be "loading up" and using far too much fuel without delivering the normal thrust. Mr. Bishop said he would take care of that too. He explained that the spark plugs were good and did not need to be changed. I asked him to see if he could relocate a forward bilge pump to a position at the rear of the bilge under the cabin as it leaves too much water there due to the attitude of the boat at rest or when running. He promised to see what he could do.

I asked whether, in his opinion, this boat would be capable of a trip down the Tennessee-Tombigbee Waterway. He replied, "I don't see why not." I immediately felt better about taking the trip as I have a deep respect for his ability as a mechanic.

I contacted Blue Springs Marina about the bottom paint and Brian said he might finish it today. He didn't know whether the rub rail and port side intake vent cowling had been repaired but promised to check and let me know.

## December 28, 2001

Today finds Spencer and me back in the woods; we're stacking dead pine trees to burn. I obtained a Roane County burn permit for the weekend and the weather is a chilly 34 degrees with a hint of a breeze. At first we rearranged an existing pile to get more distance between the brush to be burned and two lovely holly trees. The property owner, Mrs. Cole, would not be happy if we burned the pile of brush and scorched her holly bushes.

This work is hard; especially since the dead branches and trunks are entwined and are in a very deep pile. I wish we had been able to convince Mrs. Cole to let us burn the brush from the start - too late now. It took four hours of hard labor to restack the brush. After we had two fires started in the main pile we continued to toss other brush into the fire. It wasn't long until we had a large fire burning. It burned for another four hours before we became exhausted and called it a day. The tree trunk logs would burn down during the night. You can imagine how tiring this type of work can be for a couple of out-of-condition types like Spencer and me.

That evening we treated ourselves to a long soak in my Blue Springs hot tub.

## December 29, 2001

This morning we discovered the fire had burned all the wood except some of the largest pieces. Using pitchforks we are able to gather the unburned but still hot pieces into two new piles. They soon rekindled themselves and burst into flames. We fed these fires from the rest of the brush in the area and by noon our job was done. We felt good since the customer was happy with our work and we helped her to have a prettier and safer back yard. But the main reason we felt really good was that we were closer to our goal of earning extra money to spend on our trip down the river system to the Gulf of Mexico. Each dollar earned is equated to the expenses of cruising a mile of river.

By our estimate, we should now have earned enough to cover the cost of the gasoline we expect to use. Next, we will start working toward earning spending money for the trip.

After a short discussion we decided to advertise our services by printing business cards. Since people who perform odd jobs abound in our area and it seems that every other person you meet has a business card, we wanted ours to be somewhat different. We decided on this:

PINE TREE REMOVAL
(DEAD OR ALIVE)
FREE ESTIMATES
B & S TREE SPECIALISTS

## New Year's Eve, 2001

We spent this holiday at home watching Dick Clark's *Rockin' New Year* program on TV. By midnight I was only able to watch the ball drop in Times Square through slits between my eyelids then stagger off to bed. The gas pack heating system for the house is still on the blink and with a forecast low temperature of 18 degrees I banked the fireplace high with large pieces of wood in hopes our water pipes would not freeze and burst.

# January, 2002

When we awoke this morning, it was very sunny and the temperature was rising. The sun coming through the all-glass sliding doors quickly warmed the house to 60 degrees. The wood in the fireplace had burned completely so I took this opportunity to remove the mountain of ashes and hot coals that had accumulated over the last three days and nights. We were reasonably warm and cozy while we waited for the needed parts to arrive to repair the furnace.

When I mentioned to Saundra that we were saving a fortune in propane fuel costs by using the fireplace for home heating I received *that* look. You know the one.

Our hope is that we will get the parts and have the furnace repaired before I have to saw down the entire TVA woods beside our house for heating fuel. So far, we've had to use only those trees which were on our property and needed to be cut.

The morning of the third I found an especially happy email message on my computer. It was from Karen, our daughter-in-law in Boston, who informed us that there was an update concerning her pregnancy. She said a doctor's examination revealed that the date for delivery of her baby should be August 25th instead of sometime in September as she was previously told. That means she's six and a half weeks into her pregnancy. We are very happy and anxious for the new arrival. This will be our first grandchild and we're not sure how to act.

By the end of this day we are no nearer to having the heating system repaired. The fireplace is still working well and we are cozy. It feels like a very long weekend away from home at a vacation cottage in the woods.

January 4th was a bad day. I was splitting and stacking firewood for the predicted snowstorm to come this weekend when Teresa, the fiancée of Saundra's brother, Steve Grant, called. She was very distressed on the phone and told Saundra that Steve had died that morning of an apparent heart attack. It was a sad day indeed. Steve was only fifty-one years old and had recently told me that he felt better than he had felt in years.

Our attention shifted immediately to travel plans to Ohio for the funeral. Steve had been a good, kind man with malice toward none. I tried to recall if I had ever seen him angry, or heard an angry word from him about anyone. I could not recall one such incident, and I have known him for over forty years. Steve accompanied us when we brought our boat down the Ohio and up the Tennessee River in 1994 to where our new home now stands. We are very sad that he is gone but very glad that we visited him in Ohio recently and that he and Teresa found the time to visit us a few weeks ago.

The trip to Ohio was interrupted by an overnight stop at the home of my oldest sister, Glenna Boggs, in Sandy Hook, Kentucky. We arrived in Ohio on Sunday and spent as much time as we could with Steve's children, Brenda, Cathy and Brad. The funeral and interment was on Tuesday afternoon. He was laid to rest with full military honors in Coalton Cemetery. The flag from the casket was presented to his son Brad, twenty-five, who is in the US Navy Submarine Service.

It was a heart-rending ceremony and many sad tears

were shed. We will remember Steve as we cruise to Mobile Bay. I know he would have loved to be there with us.

God bless you, Steve.

On Thursday January 10, 2002 I received a telephone call from David Anderson, a neighbor and friend of Bill Griffin. Bill is the manager of the local hardware store and a fellow boater on Watts Bar Lake. Bill had told David of my trip down the rivers from Pittsburgh, Pennsylvania and he wanted to meet me to discuss long cruises on the rivers. He is planning a trip of approximately 2,000 miles to the Great Lakes this summer in a 28 foot Wellcraft with dual engines. Dave, Carol, Saundra and I will have dinner together tomorrow at Ivan's Restaurant in Rockwood. I hope to learn as much about boating from Dave as he learns from me.

Dinner was pleasant and Dave and Carol were very easy to like. They are planning a very exciting trip and are capable boaters. Both have been Coast Guard Auxiliary members and have performed courtesy safety checks on pleasure boats. I am afraid that I had little to add to their knowledge of power boating or cruising. I did tell some stories of my early days of boating and the times I made mistakes on the water.

They invited us to cruise along with them to New York via the Mississippi and the Great Lakes. We will probably decline as our trip to the gulf coast and New Orleans via the Tenn-Tom Waterway has been in the back of our minds for years and we want very much to complete it this summer.

Spencer and Caroline joined us on Sunday afternoon, January 13, to begin the process of generating a "float plan" to New Orleans. This involves studying the *Quimby's Cruising Guide* and other sources of information about the Tennessee River and the Tombigbee Waterway, or the Tenn-

Tom, as it is often referred to. Then we will use the information to print a schedule of travel and associated activities. This will be used as a general guide but will not be an ironclad schedule. This document provides all the information pertaining to anchorage locations, marinas, pump-out facilities, restaurants, fuel locations and notes of special interest or danger requiring caution while underway. This is a very useful tool and a must when a long cruise is undertaken. A copy will be left with a key person or persons who can use it to locate our party after we are underway.

After much discussion a tentative departure date of June 3, 2002 was agreed upon. A maximum daily cruising range of approximately 100 miles was established and after almost two hours of planning only four days of float plan was completed. But we all learned something about each other in the process. Two days later I completed the float plan to the northern entrance of Mobile Bay.

Spencer and I continued working in the woods cutting large yellow pines from a city lot in Rockwood, TN. Spencer is something of an expert when it comes to felling trees and is adept at dropping them in the predicted location. With some help from a friend with a Uniloader, we completed the job and collected our pay. Thus we added to the expense fund for the Cruise of a Lifetime. We hope that the need for our services will continue until we earn enough to cover the total cost of the trip.

Saundra's 60th birthday, January 19th, is a rainy day. She doesn't see her age as a reason to celebrate but I do. She still has her natural red hair, with very few gray strands around her temples. Her face is as young looking as ladies who are much younger, and she shows no wrinkles or lines to indicate her age. I still think she is very pretty. And that's reason enough for me to celebrate.

This morning our overnight guests, including my mother, brother and my oldest sister and her daughter, left for Florida. My mother was 89 years old on January 16 and has great difficulty walking, even with the help of a walker. They are taking her to my other sister's home in Florida to stay there for a while. While they were here I asked Glenna, a recent widow, whether she would enjoy a cruise to Kentucky Lake next summer. From her response I believe she would welcome the opportunity. When you start talking and planning a cruise it seems to become addictive.

We've just had a rainy three days and nights ending in a very windy night that blew trees down in many areas. The lake level rose gradually and now it is about an inch over the dock floor. The amount of debris swept into the lake was just unbelievable. It slowly floated down the lake in a giant flotilla of Christmas trees, logs, tree trunks, and once in a while a wheel and tire would go by. Styrofoam cups were plentiful as well as plastic soft drink containers.

Our dock acted as a skimmer and collected an ugly carpet of floating debris, which seems to be stuck inside the L-shaped dock. I know that when the high water recedes there will be enough wood on the edge of the lake to fuel a large bonfire. This is not unusual in the spring but a little rare this early in the year.

When you see this much flotsam it makes you wonder where it all goes and if we might encounter some of it on the way to the Gulf. I hope that it all will have found a bottom or a bank to attach to. Even better, maybe someone will pick most of it off their shoreline and burn it. Today the cloud cover is gone and a bright, sunny sky has replaced it.

Port Gillum dock at flood stage

Oh, God! It's Tuesday, the 29th of January! Where is the time going? Yesterday and today I worked with Spencer cutting, piling and then burning dead pine trees. This time (as usual) it was on a hillside with the trees on the side of a yard. I ache all over. I have soreness and pain and stiffness in all my joints and muscles. When I got home after a full day working in the seventy-degree winter day my shirt and trousers were soaked with perspiration. My face was red and covered with dust and ash from the fires we were burning.

Standing in the shower I keep telling myself that after this I will appreciate the relaxation of a summer cruise much more. Anyway the pay will help cover expenses, especially fuel, as we cruise the two thousand miles round trip to New Orleans. Our effort to find work seems to be paying off as we are now what is called *covered up* - a local term for being booked ahead.

Today I looked at a job that will involve the use of a Uniloader to pull trees away from the residence of the mayor of Midtown. This is no time to become famous in the local newspaper for destroying his home by felling a large pine tree on it. We'll use a cable or rope to pull the tree as we cut it from the stump. Tricky work on a hillside above a house - you bet!

The lake water level has dropped and left a trashy mess on my dock. I have finally convinced myself to think of the silt, debris and trash that floats down the lake during high water as a natural part of what lakes do, and it is really just nutrition for the creatures that live in it. I have a feeling that the lake will be over the boards on my dock again before we head toward the Tenn-Tom. Right now I am just hoping that when we are ready to depart the lake will show us her pretty face with clear water and fair weather. We aren't naive enough to expect perfect weather all the time, but a sunny start would really be appreciated.

## February 2002

Ground hog day came and went and left us a promise of six more weeks of winter. By now we have settled into a pattern of passing time doing the mundane things that are neither entertaining nor boring. Household chores, occasional trips to grocery stores and trash bins and the weekly square dance on Monday evening in the Harriman VFW hall help us tolerate the winter months. We have taken to short daily walks to help us lose weight and to improve our overall fitness.

The young German Shepherd dog in the new house along our road is now our fast friend. She usually greets us by a rather sheepish approach and waits for a good scratch on her head before we move along, then she returns to her guard post on the porch. At the far end of our walk *Boy* and *Bell* greet us happily. Our good friends, Dan and Helen Collier, own these dogs. Boy is a Golden Retriever and Bell is an English Setter. Both are extremely loving animals, and come running to greet us as we approach their home. Both must be petted, then they will trot happily back to their home.

Our neighbors, Dan and Helen Collier, entertained us last evening when Helen gave Saundra a belated birthday dinner. They are a gracious couple and we always enjoy their company. Dan told us of an unfortunate incident involving his pontoon boat. He said that the recent high water had raised his boat off the shoreline where he had it tied to his dock and dragged the anchor closer to the boat. When the water level went back to winter pool level one pontoon settled onto the anchor and was badly dented. No crack or hole in the pontoon could be found so that luckily it was not punctured. I'm sure the local repair staff will happily extract their pound of flesh to affect repairs. This is another example of the description of a boat as *a black hole in the water into which one throws lots of money.*

We invited Dan and Helen to join us for a cruise to Chattanooga in May of this year. It will be a shakedown cruise to check on repairs, engine performance, gas consumption rates as well as a pleasure cruise to a popular tourist destination. We have lived in Rockwood, Tennessee for seven years and have never visited Chattanooga.

Tomorrow, February 4th, will be another day of tree work for the B & S Tree Specialists. We'll be working in 25 – 30 degree weather to remove an eighty-foot tall hemlock tree from a front yard where it was blown down three weeks ago. A large amount of dirt must be dug from the roots of the stump and deposited in the hole where the tree used to be. We'll trim the limbs from the tree, drag them into a field, and pile them for burning after they dry out this fall. The large tree trunk will be sawed into logs and a neighbor will use his Uniloader to remove them. This operation should take a full day.

Tuesday we'll prune six apple trees that look like they have been totally neglected for years. The county agent's office gave me a publication about pruning that I will use as a guide. This project should take a day also. These two days represent the amount of income needed to buy fuel enough to cruise the *Saundra Kay* about four hundred miles toward New Orleans. After this job we have only one more eight-hour project lined up.

Tuesday is a day of total torture. Apple trees neglected for years become gnarled masses of twisted twigs and limbs. Rotten wood is hidden by outer growth that appears to be firm and healthy. We waited for the temperature to climb from 18 degrees in the early hours to about 30 degrees by ten thirty. This job that we thought would be relatively easy turned out to be all we could get done by five thirty. Spencer spent his day on a ladder or in the limbs wielding a chain saw. I was the director of tree surgery from the ground. My job was to direct Spencer to the limbs to cut. Then I dragged the cut limbs down through the tree to the ground and piled them up for Brad, Spencer's son, to drag to the brush pile. The bright spot of the day was that we were paid when we finished the job. We now have only two days of work contracted to do. We need more. Spencer suggested that we become chimney cleaning specialists.

Why not?

Well, here it is Saturday, the sixteenth of February and the sun is shining brightly with an expected high temperature of fifty-eight degrees. Birds are singing and calling for their prospective mates. Woodpeckers drum on hollow trees announcing their territories. Saundra and I enjoyed a refreshing dip in the hot tub while the sun climbed over the hills in the east. It's hard to think of work at a time like this but it is such a part of who we are that I just automatically start to think of what I need to do today. It's almost a sin to waste such beautiful weather staring at a TV.

The two contracted jobs are now completed and I have managed to bid and win another project for tomorrow. We don't like to work on Sunday but it is the only time Spencer will be available for over a week and the weather forecast is perfect for cutting and burning an old fallen pine tree. The customer will have a burn permit and it should not take very long to complete. And for the first time we agreed to clean a chimney as part of our contract. A few specialty items for cleaning chimneys were purchased at Potters Hardware Store and now we are ready. In the future we will include Chimney Sweeping in our service line. We have bid on two large jobs but without any positive response. Our pricing strategy for large or difficult jobs is to set the price at the level we would like to have; not necessarily what the prospective customer wants to pay. This way if we win a large job it will be worth the additional effort required of us since it involves subcontracting heavy equipment to supplement what we have. So far this has netted us only one fairly large job. But I can honestly report that all our customers have expressed satisfaction with our services.

I was wrong about this being an easy job! It turned out to be a real strange job but with a pleasant twist. When we had stacked the tree into a pile on what the customer said was her property her neighbor arrived and announced that it was *not* her property. The customer checked the plot plans for the subdivision and discovered her neighbor was correct. We had to load the brush and blocks of tree trunks onto the old truck, along with a dismantled swing set, and transport it to Spencer's place on the mountain where it will be burned later. We were paid an extra forty dollars for her error and were awarded another project to install. This time we will become *cross tie retaining wall* specialists.

My efforts on the Internet have paid off with free information packages from the cities of New Orleans and Mobile and the states of Alabama, Louisiana, and

Mississippi. It is an overwhelming chore to try to select the most desirable vacation destinations from all this information. I think we will just start the trip and decide as we go along. It will fill the time when there is nothing to see during our cruising runs. The state tourism departments of the three states I contacted have been very responsive to our need for information and if you believe the information in their pamphlets, there is <u>lots</u> to see and do. Spencer and I are especially interested in freshwater and saltwater fishing. I'm going to call for a Mississippi Gulf Coast Charter Boat Directory today.

On Monday the twenty-fifth of February, after a blustery and rainy night we, Spencer, his son Brad, and I built a cross-tie retaining wall for a lady who was interested in keeping her three dogs in her back yard. I found it difficult to believe that two men could lift used ties and carry them across a yard but we did. The job was nearly done in one day. We completed it on Tuesday and advised the property owner that her deck needed to be replaced, not repaired, as she had hoped. She asked me to provide a proposal and bid for that work too. A satisfied customer is a special reward for work well done.

On Thursday we looked at a job that involved clear-cutting a five-acre tract and burning the brush. A big job but we bid it anyway. Chances of success are probably about zero on that one. When we left, Spencer drove to the Atlanta area to visit his son and to get the really large chainsaw his son had been telling him about and for which Spencer has recently been salivating. The urge to possess large power tools is as compelling to some people as is the urge to eat or drink or make love. I think it is the same as for those who MUST HAVE that mighty, four-wheel drive SUV, just in case there is a need to go OFF-ROAD!??? Feel that power!

Well, it is true that about three months ago we did cut a tree with a rather large trunk; forty-two inches in diameter, I think. Now, if we ever run into such a tree again we will be ready. And the really important part is that Spencer will have a big smile on his face as the chainsaw throws large chips at his feet like a giant beaver with saucer sized teeth. Lumberjacks need to be happy in their work.

## March 2002

A light rain has been falling since early morning and finally has stopped. It is March 13th, and the time remaining until the departure date is down to about eleven weeks.

I've received a set of charts from Marine Navigation, Inc., which covers the northern Gulf area from Mobile Bay to the New Orleans area, including the GIWW – the Gulf Intracoastal Water Way. The total cost was $123.84.

Yesterday Saundra and I visited the Knoxville store of Boat World, Inc. and purchased a Weems & Plath Primary Navigation Set, a Super Hooker #13 anchor, one shackle, a chart tube, floating key ring, throwable cushion floatation device, two power cord support straps and last, but not least, a stainless steel fish and veggie grill tray for our Magma BBQ grill. This tray will be used, we hope, to cook the many fish we plan to catch along the way. Saundra also found a nice folding table to use in the cockpit when snacks and drinks are served. This eliminated the need to use the larger convertible table from the cabin.

Our list of items still needed for the boat is now much smaller. We still have to address the issue of new flares, lines, anchor rodes, and fenders. A quick review of the nautical charts of the Gulf shows that water beyond the offshore islands has a typical depth of forty feet. Thus a normal seven to one scope would require 280 feet of anchor rode. A short scope of three to one would only require 120 feet of rode. I am starting to think that a 250 foot roll of ½ inch nylon would be perfect for the back-up anchor, a 120 foot rode on the primary anchor carried on the anchor platform would be a good combination. The Super Hooker is a Danforth type anchor and is recommended for all bottom types except rocky bottoms.

A quick perusal of the charts from Marine Navigation, Inc. was very instructional. First, I realized that I have a lot to learn about reading and using nautical charts, not to mention understanding all the symbols displayed there. Now I wish that I had attended the Power Squadron course on piloting and navigation. But I intend to study all the information available to me now, and to augment that with whatever is available in the bookstores and library. For the very limited off shore cruising we are likely to do in the Gulf, I doubt that I will need to be a qualified navigator. We won't be more than 25-30 miles offshore at any time and certainly not in bad weather or at night. My boat is not really large enough and the fuel capacity is insufficient to allow me to cruise at any distance from shore facilities. She is top heavy and has only a nine foot, six inch beam so she will roll more easily than a boat with a lower center of gravity.

## "Too much loft"

Friday March 15, at 9:20 a.m., after a lengthy preparation and loading sequence, we were finally ready to board our aging Honda Accord Coupe and hit the road; destination – Tampa, Florida. We arrived at Peach Tree City, GA in time for dinner with our son James and his wife, Paulette. In the morning we continued south to Summerfield, FL where my mother lives with my sister, Madeline Conn. On Monday we continued southwest toward Tampa and arrived in the New Port Richie, FL area where our good friends, Ray and Janet Cass have chosen to retire in a gated golf community. Their white, one-story stucco executive estate home is neatly and conveniently situated within 100 feet of the 12th green of their golf course.

It is pure pleasure to sit on their screened-in porch called a "lanai" and watch golfers agonize over putts on the green. Houses here look alike with slight variations. They completely surround the course and are about 20 feet apart. This closeness is both a nuisance for the lack of privacy and a boon for the tendency to have increased social intercourse and group activities with your neighbors.

I enjoyed three rounds of golf with Ray while Saundra and Janet chose to shop the area stores and use the excellent facilities of the community center. During one of the golf rounds I was informed of the reason that one of my tee shots had barely reached the far shore of a lake in front of the tee.

One of Ray's friends in our foursome told me that my problem was loft. "Loft, what do you mean, loft"? I asked. He replied, "Loft, you know, L-O-F-T, Lack Of Friggin' Talent!" Well, it's true; I swing a golf club the same way a

Georgia prisoner on a road gang uses a swing blade to cut weeds.

Anyway, the golfing was very enjoyable and Ray's friends were very nice and easy to like. We spent five wonderful days with Ray and Janet before we headed back north on Friday morning. Again we stayed with James and Paulette in Peach Tree City Friday night until Monday morning.

On the way home we stopped in Chattanooga to check out the downtown area and to locate Ross' Landing Marina. It was a new facility on the left side down-bound just below the municipal landing where the *Southern Belle* docks. Randy Jones is the operator of the Marina. It was 6:10 a.m. when we arrived home. Our trip was a really enjoyable one and one that we will remember. But, as always, it was good to be home again.

Thursday, March 27, is a sunny day with temperatures rising into the seventies. It is a good day to check on another potential opportunity to earn money for the cruise. Saundra agreed to accompany me on a trip to evaluate the job and meet the customer. It turned out to be the parents of the owner of the property who we met to discuss the scope of the work. The elderly gentleman, who is within days of his 80th birthday, spoke with a rather heavy Italian accent. He explained that he was an immigrant fifty years ago and has been operating a large dairy farm in New York for most of his adult life. His physical size belied the work that he described because he was a very short man, no more than 5'4" tall but his hands were the hands of a man who had done a lifetime of hard work.

His wife was even shorter than he at about 4'10" and a very jolly and pleasant lady. He arrived in this country with

$50.00 in his pocket and built a productive life here, raised a family, produced dairy products and employed others on his two farms. This is what America is all about. We must have chatted for a half-hour before we took a look at the work needed - to clear falling and dead pine trees from around this, his daughter's house.

We continued our travels and arrived at the Blue Springs Marina to check on the status of the *Saundra Kay*. She had been hauled and her bottom painted a wild color of bright blue with big blotches of darker blue. She was *stack stored* on a rack near the roof of the building so I couldn't inspect her closely to find out what the repairs on her rub rail looked like. Based on the appearance of the bottom paint, I feel a little leery. But that won't make her less seaworthy, which is the really important thing. I made a mental note to check on other marinas for any further repairs requiring hull work and arranged to take delivery of my boat on the first of May.

Saundra is concerned that we will be cramped for time to get the boat ready for the trip. Surely Spencer and I can clean a boat in a month of weekends and evenings. Besides, we would prefer washing and waxing a boat to cutting and burning dead pine trees any day!

## April 2002

My golfing experience in Florida is beginning to pay off in new and unexpected ways. My lower back has begun to hurt beyond endurance, so I can't help Spencer in the woods today, April 2nd. It is a result of a poor lie on the first drive of the day and when I took my second shot from a steep bank in the rough with one foot much lower than the other, I felt something strange happen to my lower back muscles. By the end of the second hole I was sure my back would be sore for some time. It hasn't improved, probably because I tried to continue as if nothing was wrong. Now I am paying for it.

Today was sunny with a slight southwest breeze. We lay in the sun on our deck for the first time this year. We'll need to be tanned before we start to Mobile Bay. Since we are fair-skinned redheads, we need to take it slowly.

April 12, 2002 promises to be a warm day in the low seventies with possible light showers and periods of sunlight. The dogwood blossoms are near their peak, and our woods are dappled with the white petals. The lake is near summer pool level and I am starting to believe that it will be left up for the summer season with no appreciable drawdown. My lower back is still very tender and I have been unable to participate actively in the wood cutting activities with Spencer. Tonight we are getting together to review our plans for the cruise, and to finalize the financial arrangements. The recent rise in fuel costs is a concern and must be factored into the budget. We want to be able to cruise without any impact on our regular incomes. And we must plan for cessation of activities in the woods and for beginning to outfit and equip the boat for the cruise. We have arranged to take delivery of the *Saundra Kay* on May first at Blue Springs Marina. Our marine mechanic, Carey Bishop, will give the boat a final inspection.

Our crew had a meeting on the twelfth and arrived at hardly any hard decisions except that Carolyn will be the keeper of the records of expenses during our cruise. She is visiting a bank on Monday to determine the safest method of transporting funds. We think it probably will be best to use credit cards and money orders instead of cash for most of our transactions. The best thing that came out of our discussions was that we decided to pool all the funds and use them without consideration as to individual expenditures. Until all the money is gone, it belongs to anyone who wants to use it for something along the way. We all contributed and will all use it as though it were our own. Let's see how this works out. If we come home as friends, we'll call President Bush and advise him on how to mediate the mid-east crisis.

The IRS should be happier now that I have finished computing my income tax and again I had to use the white label on the envelope indicating that I owed taxes. And I had thought I had the system figured out so I would break even. Tomorrow is the fifteenth of April and I slid under the wire once again.

My back is still sore but much better and I am beginning to think I may recover. I'm going to try to work in the woods again tomorrow and Tuesday. The wood ticks have begun to be a problem and some have tried to make me their home. Saundra said that I should leave my clothes outside when I return from the woods. That should make for an interesting situation.

As for snakes, we have yet to encounter one in the woods. But we know they are there, copperheads and rattlers as well as the harmless kinds. We will make lots of noise and stay alert.

Saundra has not been feeling well and is getting tired easily. She had some pain in her upper chest last evening after working in the house all day. I told her to rest today and to get help to do her house cleaning for a while. I will try to relieve some of the stress of planning the boat cleanup and preparation for the cruise. She is scheduled to see her doctor soon and is talking to her nurse practitioner about her condition. I am worried about her.

April 21 is sunny and warm and the lake is still at near summer levels. We've had record setting temperatures this month with highs near ninety. Tomorrow is supposed to be more normal with temperature highs returning to the seventies. We're getting excited about having the boat home from storage and starting to get her ready for the cruise. Spencer and I plan to complete one final contract of wood clearing and then 'retire' until some undetermined time in the future after we return from New Orleans.

Next weekend Saundra and I are traveling to Kennesaw, GA to assist our son Mike with his new house inspection since he cannot be there. My lower back pain is getting much better so I should be able to tolerate the trip now. I have been able to work in the woods and in the flower garden. Saundra still tires easily but is better than she was. She is buoyed up by the happy news that James and Paulette announced that they are going to try to adopt a baby plus the expected arrival of our first grandchild in August. Mike and Karen want to be settled in their new home in Kennesaw before their baby's arrival.

Ospreys are our special birds around here and are showing off their new offspring. They must have nested just up the lake again this year. Earlier we watched them struggle to tear twigs directly from standing trees while in forward flight and carry them toward their nest site. Sometimes the load is more than their wings can support but they valiantly try against all odds. Sometimes they have to drop their load just before they plummet into the lake. I've seen them struggle into a strong headwind with a small limb in their talons and appear to stand still. Eventually the limb is dropped and the bird flies off to search for a load that it can handle. The young birds are in training now and emit plaintive cries overhead as they soar and dive with their parents. They are beautiful in flight and seem to be able to soar endlessly on the slightest breeze.

Two large white oak trees flank our house and are almost fully leafed out now. The yellow pollen has covered everything around here for the last three weeks and now the small strands of dried blossoms have floated down upon us and the roof looks like it is covered with a thin layer of this light brown fluff. When it rains and washes the roof it will stick along the edges of the gutters in small clumps of spongy debris. It makes good mulch to use on potted plants. I can't think of any other use for it.

All this pollen has taken its toll on Spencer. His eyes are swollen, his voice is hoarse and he coughs in violent wrenching fits until his breath is gone. Then, red faced and teary eyed, he says he thinks he is getting better. We need a good rain to clear the air of all this pollen and wash the junk off all the roofs. Rain is predicted for today or tonight but it

106

appears to have passed us by for now. It's only four in the afternoon so we still have a chance.

Today I swept the debris off the roof of the house and collected a large amount of the fuzzy brown stuff oak trees drop in the early spring. Rain has swept the pollen from the air and the leaves on the trees are nearly fully formed. Reports of tornado warnings in southeastern Kentucky and the cloudy skies make us keep a weather eye.

If all goes well I will get the *Saundra Kay* from Blue Springs Marina on Monday and bring her home. We plan to go to Chattanooga on the 18th of May for an overnighter trial run with our neighbors Dan and Helen Collier and stay at Ross's Landing Marina. It will be a short stay there but since the cruise will be about 200 miles and four locks it should be a good test of the state of readiness of boat and crew.

Saundra is getting very anxious to start preparing the boat for the trip to New Orleans. After all, it's only about a month until departure.

Monday is a clear and sunny day after a weekend of tornado watches and thunderstorm warnings with heavy winds. I called Blue Springs Marina and arranged to have our boat taken from dry storage and put into the water.

Spencer came to my home and Saundra drove us to the marina. We took the boat and filled her with gasoline and pumped her waste holding tank. The gas cost $1.65/9 per gallon and the pumpout was free. Saundra drove the car home while Spencer and I took the boat. We idled through the no-wake zone and out into the lake. The engine sounded smooth and powerful while idling and when we increased the speed to 3,700 RPM we were quickly on plane. We were very happy to have the engine performing so well.

The *Saundra Kay* is now riding at anchor beside our dock so that she won't be damaged by high wakes from large cruisers going by.

## May, 2002

Bad news arrived on the evening of May third. Saundra answered the phone at about four-thirty and Carolyn was on the line. She had returned from a visit to her doctor. He had diagnosed the pain in her right foot to be a result of a bone fracture. The bone showed signs of mending and new calcium deposits could be seen on the x-rays at the point of the fracture. He recommended using a hinged boot and keeping her weight off the foot for approximately six weeks.

Since we plan to begin our cruise in four weeks we are all concerned about the advisability of such an undertaking for someone with a mending fracture of the foot. Her doctor advised Carolyn that she should be able to make the trip if she could keep her foot elevated most of the time. Carolyn is so determined to make this cruise that she is convinced that in a month she will be healed and ready to go.

It has been raining since the boat has been home so no work has been done to clean her up. The lake water level is above normal pool and the water is against the dock floor joists. After a sunny day tomorrow more rain is predicted. It appears that the trip to Chattanooga might be in jeopardy unless we get a major change in the weather pattern. We met with Dan and Helen last evening for dinner and to plan the details. Everyone seemed anxious to get the boating season started.

Sunday May 5, 2002 is a slow starter. Clouds in the morning are finally chased away by noon, a sunny afternoon arrives, and the temperature rises to 78 degrees. Saundra and I get the boat positioned alongside the dock, which by now is only about eight inches above the water. The cleaning tools and cleaners are positioned on the dock and ready for Spencer's arrival just after 2:00 p.m. By six o'clock the exterior of the hull is cleaned and the cockpit has been scrubbed. Saundra has removed the bedding that has become wet in spots and it is drying on the dock.

Apparently the replacement of the rub rail along the port side aft (two six foot lengths) was not caulked properly. Traces of the water leaks could be easily seen on the inside of the boat from the rub rail down the bulkheads to the bedding cushions. We decided to advise Blue Springs Marina of the poor work on Monday. Meantime we will get a tube of caulk and try to stop the leaks by caulking the rub rails without removing them. I hope that Blue Springs Marina will step up and apply a permanent fix. At this point I am unsure that their repair yard is up to the task.

Another bit of bad news came early yesterday when I received a call from my brother-in-law telling me that my mother is in the hospital in Florida being treated for an infection. She is eighty-nine years old and in poor health. We all hope she will get well soon and back to her home in Summerfield.

The *Saundra Kay* is showing her age a little bit more than I expected. On the seventh of May Spencer and I worked on the boat again. This time we tackled the marine head, in particular the Jabsco manual flush toilet. It has been loose from the deck and some leakage has been noticed. One of the hold-down screws has broken the flange off the base and is not able to secure the toilet bowl base to the deck. There is not enough space in this head to think much less to be able

110

to disassemble a defective toilet assembly. We washed everything and sanitized the toilet before we began to take it apart. It was not a pretty sight, but with much effort and patience we were able to repair and replace the defective unit. The only cost was elbow grease and some plumbers caulk. When we tried to use the pumpout for the shower it was very slow, nearly inoperative. Inspection of the pump in the engine compartment showed that the filter in the line ahead of the pump was clogged with the same stuff you would find in your home shower drain. Once removed, the pump worked well.

The sliding cabin windows on port and starboard side have metal trim at the aft end. This trim anchors the sheet of glass and secures it when it is closed. I noticed that the metal strips were loose and removed them from the pane of glass before they fell into the water. I'm sure they would have been very difficult to replace. Inspection showed that the original factory glue had failed causing the metal trim to become detached from the glass. Spencer cleaned the glass and the metal trim, applied plumbers Goop and glued them back together. A quick, hard summer shower wet us down, cooled us off and exposed a leak in the forward hatch cover.

The opaque "sheet plastic" hatch cover had become loose from its frame in one corner. After the water dried off, a thin bead of clear caulk was applied all around the hatch cover. Another job well done by Spencer! The waste system was evaluated for the best way to modify it to comply with the Coast Guard regulations which stipulate that all through-hull fittings must be plugged. Waste cannot be pumped overboard. Although I strictly use pump-out facilities, my boat's waste system was designed to also pump overboard. No easy lockable shutoff valve is in this system so I have no way to comply but to find a way to plug the through-hull fitting. I'll call the experts tomorrow. The forward navigational lights, green and red, are not working. Two of the courtesy lights in the cockpit are inoperative. That is tomorrow's work.

The Yard Dog lawn service didn't come again today and the grass shows it. More rain at noon just added fuel to the fire. How high will it be before it is cut? When will it quit raining long enough to dry out? The forecast doesn't give much promise of a dry day for a while. Rather than succumb to the temptation to cut the grass myself I will try to wait out the wet weather and the absence of Yard Dog. I just have to train myself to relax no matter what happens or how long it takes. This is Friday, May 10, and only 23 days remain until we shove off toward New Orleans.

I returned some articles of square dance clothing to Judy Speer today. Judy and Charley are our neighbors in Pin Oak Pointe. They recently returned from a long vacation trip to Alaska by camper truck and Judy is planning a church sponsored trip to Venezuela in July. Charley is a very good bass fisherman and is a member of a bass fishing club in this area. He is familiar with the use of a GPS for positioning and locating fishing hot spots or *fishin' holes* as he calls them. We discussed the relative value of using a GPS on the river and Charley's report was not all good. In fact, he told a story about being on the water but according to the GPS display, his boat was about 150 yards up in the woods. That didn't make Charley very fond of that technology.

A check of the boat running and courtesy lights revealed three bulbs were burned out, including the bow red/green running light. Two courtesy lights had burned out bulbs and all three courtesy lights had lenses that had been darkened from clear to amber/brown by the UV rays of the sunlight. I took the bad bulbs to Central Automotive in Harriman, Tennessee. They sell boats and boat accessories and are quite helpful. I bought replacement bulbs and ordered replacement courtesy light fixtures. They should be in by next Tuesday.

Mother's Day weekend went well. Jamey spent Saturday and Sunday with us and Mike and Joe called and chatted for awhile. Jamey and I played nine holes of golf at Southwest Point Golf Course in Kingston. He shot par 37 and I shot lots more (57). I was just glad that my lower back pain didn't return during or after the round.

I called my mother in Florida to wish her a happy mother's day. She is 89 and just back from the hospital where she was treated for a severe infection. She is feeling better and getting around the house with the aid of a walker.

On Monday Saundra is not feeling too well. Her blood pressure is finally down to the normal range but her pulse is only 55, low for her. She doesn't look well and she is reporting dizziness too. She will call her nurse practitioner this morning to discuss her situation. I am concerned that the treatment for high blood pressure is driving things to the extreme in the opposite direction.

Late Sunday afternoon our neighbors, Dan and Helen Collier invited us to go with them on their shakedown cruise of their pontoon boat. We gladly accepted and they picked us up at our dock and we cruised for about fifteen miles around Thief Neck Island and into Crystal Cove. The lake was choppy but not so much as to make it ride rough. The pontoon slid easily over the chop without throwing any spray. This was Saundra's first venture on the lake this season. We hope to cruise to Chattanooga next weekend, the

18th of May, for an overnight stay with Dan and Helen on our boat. Helen has planned the activities and seems quite excited about the cruise. The latest weather forecast for this week shows a 70% chance of thunderstorms for next Saturday. I just hope that the storms hold off during the time we will be on the water. We certainly have had our share of wet weather in the last three weeks.

Saundra is feeling better this evening. She contacted her doctor and discussed her medication and he decided to have her monitor her blood pressure more often and report any readings that seem out of limits. It may be that her blood pressure has been above normal for so long that it will take a long time for her system to become accustomed to the lower blood pressure.

# At last! Our shakedown cruise to Chattanooga!

Rainy, windy and cold! And dark, too! That's how it felt on the morning of the 18th of May when we began our cruise to Chattanooga. It was Saturday at 6:30 in the morning and I was on my dock preparing our boat. First I had to remove the storage tarp I had secured over her foredeck and fly bridge to protect her from tree debris. The water churned against the dock making it uncomfortable to take the paddleboat under her bow to untie the bungee cord tiedowns. I was thankful that the rain had stopped but the whitecaps on the lake made me wonder whether this was a good time to go out at all. Clouds covered the sky and I couldn't rule out the possibility that weather forecasters were wrong. No rain was forecast for today; just cold (40's) and windy. Dan and Helen Collier arrived at 6:30 a.m. and showed no reluctance to start our cruise. We soon began loading our gear, and by 7:30 a.m. we were underway.

The water was rough and covered with whitecaps and the wind occasionally whistled as it rushed by the radio antenna. Dan and I stayed on the fly bridge all the way to Chattanooga in heavy coats and caps pulled down over our eyes. We arrived at Watts Bar Lock and Dam at about 8:15 a.m. and called the lockmaster. He told us he was letting a small craft out and we could enter in about five minutes. When we entered I overshot my tie up point on the starboard side and finally got tied on the next try. I was rusty and needed more practice in windy conditions. We proceeded toward Chickamauga Lock and in some areas of long reaches the water was very choppy with white capped waves jarring our spines. The strong wind kept us in jackets and windbreakers as the cold stayed with us since the sun never shined through the clouds.

We were wearing layers of jackets, sweaters, T shirts and windbreakers but it still felt like a deer-hunting trip in the north gone bad. Our faces were red with the effects of the wind and cold. Helen tried to lift our spirits by handing up a dish of fruit snacks to eat as we just kept cruising into the cold wind. It was during this portion of the cruise that Helen made her way into the tiny marine head to do things that people need to do, even on a bouncing boat. According to her report, at some point in the process she was bent over and turned (probably to use the manual pump) and her bare bottom contacted the door that, to her mortification and shock, flew open. Luckily there were no witnesses to this X-Rated bare bottom scene! I believe Helen has now found that there is a lock on the door.

The Chickamauga Lock was preparing to let a small craft exit when we called. The lockmaster told us the lock would be ready for us in about fifteen minutes. When we entered, the wind was buffeting and we had difficulty tying to the floating bitt. I even pulled the boat alongside a stationary bitt and asked Dan to tie us to it. He said he couldn't and told me of my mistake. The lockmaster also reminded me that the floating bitts were marked with yellow paint. I was just so busy trying to get the boat close to the wall that I didn't pay attention to the real target. We proceeded to the correct bitt and tied up without much trouble this time. I was just a little bit rusty at handling the boat in a breeze. I'm glad we didn't wind up hanging from the lock wall as the water went out of the lock!

We exited the lock at about one o'clock and covered the

three miles to Chattanooga in a few minutes. The scenery along the shore shows some of the industry of the city and as you approach the municipal pier the old city shows her art district on a high limestone bluff. The beautiful aquarium is close to the pier and clearly visible from the river.

By one-thirty we were tied up to the fuel dock of Ross's Landing Marina. This marina is still under construction and not officially opened but the slips are completed and operational. Only the office area is still being finished. Our reservations for a transient slip for the night could not be confirmed immediately since there was no dock master to be found. A construction worker explained that we could take any empty slip, so we tied up in a covered one. I found that my power inlet was broken internally but I was still able to connect to shore power. (Another item to repair before going to New Orleans). The new restrooms were locked, as were the security gates. People have been climbing around the gates to get to their boats and said that nobody was there to unlock the gates for them. Saundra was quite upset and talked to the construction foreman about it. He finally gave me the key to the bathrooms and the gate and told me to just leave them under a boat lift control panel when we left. I promised to keep the restrooms locked when we weren't using them since he was concerned about unauthorized people using them for inappropriate purposes ... drugs, sex, Rock-N-Roll??

We spent the afternoon and evening in Chattanooga touring the waterfront, the art district and the Chattanooga Choo-Choo historic district. We had reservations at the Station House Restaurant for six o'clock. Our meal there was very enjoyable and the singing waiters added a special touch. A 15% additional "entertainment tax" is automatically added to the prices on the menu and is really worth it. A small band accompanied the singers on a balcony and there were different raised eating areas, which added to the ambiance. This was prom night for a lot of area students and we saw lots of them in their tuxedos and gowns around the restored train station. Horse drawn carriages offered tours for $40.00 per couple. Helen and Saundra explored the small shops, which abound in the Station area. We took the shuttle bus back to the waterfront area and walked to the boat, prepared our bunks and turned in for the night.

In the morning Helen said she hadn't slept well because she kept trying to fall out of bed. She explained that the dinette tabletop, which makes up the berth, kept sliding toward the passageway whenever she moved. I asked Helen, "Didn't you use the latch"? To which she replied, "What latch"? Another lesson learned. Poor Helen! Half a night's sleep lost needlessly.

Helen and Dan Collier on board the *Saundra Kay*

What a great couple to cruise with! Dan and Helen Collier are enthusiastic and anxious to help and are fun to be around. Dan navigated and kept me in the channel while I was busy piloting through the rough water, and handled the bumpers and lines in the locks and during docking. Helen was great to have aboard! She needed a real break from her surgical nurse duties and concerns with grandchildren's health problems. She said that this trip was like a vacation for her. We can all agree that it is hard to think about personal things when you are busy wondering if the next whitecap is hiding a half-submerged log that might split your boat in half.

On our return trip Sunday it was pleasant, cool with sunny skies but the water was very rough again with high waves and lots of whitecaps. In one long reach the water appeared the color of weak coffee with roiling rows of foam on the top. There was only one way to run these stretches and that was on full plane at 3,700 RPM, throwing spray in a wide arc on each side of the boat. The waves were spaced so that only occasionally we would crash into the side of a wave that would shake us and make a loud slapping noise. Most of the time we were able to ride the crests in a rough but rocking motion; it was exhilarating!

Dan took the helm above the Watts Bar Dam and piloted the boat up the lake to an area of wide water below Thief Neck Island, where he pulled into a cove across from Blue Springs Marina to anchor. I got the Magma propane grill fired up and grilled pork shops for a much-delayed lunch/dinner. After eating we proceeded to home port and arrived about six p.m. We were all tired and I was sunburned, but it has been a special weekend with our good friends. We hope we can cruise together again soon.

## May, 2002

### Load the Boat, Sink or Float

One week to go till departure. Saundra has been very busy getting our wardrobes together, and believe me when I say that she is dedicated to her task. Piles of clothes cover various pieces of furniture around the house as she carefully selects just the right articles to take. I know that when she is done we will have everything we need on board.

I have not been totally inactive since I am responsible for preparing the boat for the trip. Small defects we found have been cleared. The broken shore power plug has been replaced with the help of Raymond Cass, Jr. who was visiting us before starting his week of bass fishing at Lakeside Resort. I am putting a coat of topside paint on the underside of the insulated lid of the live well to seal the insulation. Then it will be covered with heavy-duty aluminum foil to assist in retaining the cold temperatures since it will be used as an icebox during at least the first part of the cruise. The Marine Kettle propane grill was cleaned and tested and the three cockpit courtesy light fixtures have been replaced. 12V electric fans have been installed in the cabin and "V" berths, since we are not air-conditioned, as the temperatures in Louisiana are sure to be high. Today will be a good day to work on the teak trim and finish the painting of the live well lid. Our two deep-cycle marine batteries will be left on trickle charge until we leave.

Last evening we had dinner at Ivan's Restaurant with Dave and Carol Anderson and their son Reed. We discussed our plans for the cruise and Dave and Carol decided to accept our invitation to join us on the first leg of our cruise as far as Chattanooga. They don't have their boat in the water yet since Dave is still trying to fix a problem with the cooling system in one of the engines. He plans to be able to launch on Tuesday after Memorial Day weekend. Dave has a GPS and offered to let me use it while we are under way to check my speed/RPM ratio. This will be valuable information for me since my speedometer is inoperative. I will be able to create a chart showing the speed generated by any setting on my tachometer. With this information I should be able to accurately calculate cruising time between points.

Saundra still is working on the wardrobe selection for the cruise. Thirty days is a long time to be away on a small boat. Storage space, weight and comfort are major factors in the selection process but according to Saundra, style and appearance are also critical. I am beginning to think that when all the clothing is taken aboard we will look like a small department store. We may just sink at our dock due to overloading. I'm keeping my mouth shut about this and staying out of the process as much as I can.

Monday, Memorial Day 2002 started with the prediction of 30% chance of thunderstorms in the afternoon. Spencer and his son, Brad, showed up to help me split and stack some firewood I had piled at the edge of my lot. Brad started fishing from the dock while I finished cutting the new growth of brush from my Boston ivy back yard. This is a twice-yearly chore that I must perform or be overcome by the fast-growing bushes and honeysuckle vines. We were all soon busily splitting the wood with a gas powered splitter and stacking the wood into three stacks about five feet high and sixteen feet long. It was a hot job and the eighty-three degree temperature didn't help. We finished just before the lightning started flashing. The storm went around us to the south and east and not a single raindrop fell on us.

Saundra spent another day sorting, selecting and ironing clothes for the trip. Tomorrow Carolyn and Saundra plan to install screens on the boat's cabin windows.

It's Tuesday, May 28, 2002, and the ladies are in the boat by 8:45 a.m. busily preparing the cabin for better air circulation and ventilation. I think they are very anxious to get started because they show a special excitement. Anticipation increases the excitement level and enjoyment of any trip to a new destination. The weather report promises rain for the day of departure but we hope that it will be the typical afternoon thundershowers which cool things down and last for a short time. If we leave at an early hour, 7:30 a.m. for example, we will have traveled through two pools and be below Chattanooga by early afternoon.

Wednesday is a bright and sunny morning. Only a small haze of fog lies near the surface of the lake. Rain upstream has raised the water level overnight and our paddle boat is trapped under the dock; held against the joists by the water. Again the weather predictions for Monday have changed. Now, sunny and hot, 87 degrees, is predicted. We are more prepared for the trip now. I changed the crankcase oil in the boat and replaced the oil filter. The two-amp trickle charge keeps the batteries at full charge. Carolyn and Saundra installed a temporary screen over the port side cabin windows then ran out of Velcro. The teak wood trim still is not refinished but I plan to work on that today. Our phone doesn't work for some reason. Static is all you can hear.

Nothing is all you can hear now on the phone. I used the cell phone to call for repairs. With luck a repairman will be out in a few days. In the meantime I checked the network interface unit and when I tilted it, blue-green water poured out. I found that it was full of rainwater - what a time for this to happen! Also, an order we placed with Overtons a week ago has not arrived. Two double stainless steel fender racks and a ring buoy will help us manage the four fenders we plan to have on board and the ring buoy can only add to our safety factor. According to the sales clerk, it should not have taken more than two or three days for the order to be delivered. It has been seven days. If it doesn't arrive tomorrow, Friday, it will be too late. We'll be underway when the package arrives. Today is Thursday, May 30, 2002. We have three more days until we leave. Saundra and I loaded our clothing into our section of the boat this afternoon and I was surprised to find there was room for more. I poured twenty gallons of fuel in the tank today so that we will be able to leave our dock with a full tank. This will save time and money. Tomorrow is grocery-shopping day for Carolyn and Saundra; it should be interesting since they haven't planned the menu yet.

It's Friday, May 31, 2002, and the groceries (provisions) for the first leg of the cruise are piled on the living room floor and the perishables are stored in the refrigerator and freezer. I am now firmly convinced that the boat will sink at dockside due to overloading!

The first stages of panic are starting to set in. Carolyn and Spencer arrived this evening with a large load of clothing and articles to put on board. Today was Spencer's last day at Potters Hardware Store as a full time employee.

After our trip he plans to work there only part time. Carolyn came to the boat after Spencer and I carried most of their articles to the dock. She began to stow the clothing in the bow when a number of wakes rocked the boat. Caroline began to get the symptoms of seasickness right away. It affected her so much that she had to leave the boat to regain her composure. She nearly lost her dinner but managed to keep it down. We all hope that this is not a preview of things to come.

Tomorrow we have some small things to do such as packing the meats and food that must be refrigerated or kept in iced coolers. We want to have everything done so that we can take only our personal toilet articles to the boat on Monday and leave the dock at 7:30 a.m. precisely.

Saundra, as always, is the one who keeps the steady hand on the wheel. She has managed to get a lot of stuff on board and in a very organized manner. When we leave we will be completely provisioned for an extended stay on the boat. We will need to dock for supplies such as water, gas, bread and milk.

Sunday, Carolyn visited her elderly mother, then she and Spencer arrived late in the afternoon with a few last minute items. At one in the afternoon I saw Dave and Carol Anderson returning from Chattanooga aboard their twenty-eight foot Wellcraft. They stopped briefly to report that the boat was running well and that their fuel economy was very good. I told them we would be leaving at seven thirty in the morning. They said they would leave at seven o'clock to meet us as we started our cruise. They intend to go back to Chattanooga to give their boat a real shakedown run.

By the end of the day everything was done except loading the frozen food, ice and personal grooming items.

At seven-thirty in the morning we will start our thirty-day 'trip of a lifetime' as Spencer has named it. Of course, we called our three sons and their wives, and my mother to say goodbye. Our friends Miguel and Marge stopped by to wish us *bon voyage*, as did our neighbor Joe Cable. Saundra's special friend and our neighbor Helen Collier came by earlier in the day and gave Saundra a swan she had painted on a special gourd and some seashells with candles. John Jolly had stopped by earlier in the week to wish a safe and pleasant trip. We will miss our good neighbors and friends while we are gone.

# Cruising the Rivers

## The Saundra Kay

## Log Two

Rockwood, Tennessee to New Orleans, Louisiana
(and back again)

June 3, 2002 to June 27, 2002

# Boat On The Cruise

The *Saundra Kay* - 25 foot Bayliner Sierra 2556
Command Bridge cabin cruiser
w/flying bridge and Bimini top
Powered by 7.4L Mercruiser I/O w/Bravo 2 Outdrive
Fuel- Gasoline (102 gallon capacity)
Range - 100 miles

*Crew*
Captain: Bill Gillum
First Mate: Saundra Gillum
Able-bodied Seamen: Spencer and Carolyn Whalen

# June 3, 2002

Rockwood, Tennessee
HOME at Mile 559.6RDB

On June third it begins at 7:30 a.m., with final loading of supplies until the last second before we cast off. Dave and Carol Anderson arrive in their boat with another couple and we cruised together toward the Watts Bar Dam. I used Dave's GPS to check my cruising speed and found it to be about 22 miles per hour. We idled through the *half moon* cut-off and met Dave on the other side. We said goodbye to the Andersons and other friends and locked through the Watts Bar Lock without any trouble. Chickamauga Lock was reached by noon, and we idled in without delay. Spencer is now in charge of tying the boat to the floating bollard or bitt and securing the fenders alongside as needed. Carolyn is assigned the task of guarding the bow from damage during locking through, and pushing us away once we are given the signal to leave the lock. Saundra is in charge of the operations in the stern of the boat during lockages, and uses a boat hook to guard against damage to the boat during locking through procedures. I run the engine and bring the boat alongside the bollard for tying, and communicate by radio with the Lockmaster. We will use this procedure for the entire trip so that everyone knows exactly what to do. This time Spencer had to make some adjustments to the line attached to the bollard and the Lockmaster reminded me to shut down the engine while in the lock. The remainder of the locking procedure went normally, and we exited the lock and cruised the five miles to Ross's Landing Marina at Chattanooga. It is located just downstream of the municipal park where the paddleboat *Southern Belle* is moored, and is very close to the aquarium.

The dock attendant told us that the waste pump-out was broken and inoperative, still. We pumped sixty gallons of fuel at $1.499 per gallon. The 95-degree heat and humidity was oppressive, so we went ashore to the Chattanooga Visitors Center to cool off. This facility is very near the Aquarium and lots of shops and restaurants are nearby. Across the street we found a homemade ice cream shop and enjoyed large cones on the way back to the boat. It was about five in the evening when we headed on down the Nickajack to a point at about Mile #434.5RDB (right descending bank). Dinner was mainly barbecued pork chops done on the propane grill. Delicious! Spencer and I tried a little fishing but came up empty.

After dinner and clean up, we prepared for our first night on the boat. The heat and humidity were felt and we were thankful that we had DC fans (3) in the boat to help keep us cool. Without them, it would have been extremely difficult to sleep aboard during the 90+ degree heat with high humidity.

# June 4, 2002

Mile #434RBD
To
Goat Island, Tennessee
Mile # 352RDB

Tuesday arrived with a fog that is lifting by seven o'clock. We had breakfast after what all agreed was a hot night. Today promises more of the same. Our anchorage was in a strong current when we dropped anchor, and there was lots of fishing activity around us. During the night, lights from a passing barge and from many fishing boats kept us from deep sleep. Because of the boats and the heat and the newness of sleeping on board our first night wasn't restful. I wondered whether this might be the beginning of a trip from Hell?

Spencer dived into the water to refresh himself and I, coward that I am, lowered myself into the lake by the swim ladder. The ladies stayed aboard. The swift current of last night had disappeared totally and we could feel the control that the locks have on the river system.

Soon after our water antics we hoisted the anchor, another job that Spencer has been assigned, and we picked our way through three miles of floating logs, limbs, chunks and unknown articles to the Hales Bar Resort and Marina. Gasoline was $1.789 per gallon, and the attendant wasn't there. The place looked somewhat abandoned but there were new covered slips in one area. Above the remains of the old lock, the docks where old houseboats were moored didn't look too well maintained. Someone finally arrived at the fuel dock but we decided to continue through the Nickajack lock and into Guntersville Lake without buying fuel we felt was too expensive.

Spencer has the locking through process down to a science, securing the line to the floating bollard efficiently. Saundra is the first mate in charge of all activities in the cockpit of the boat. She took the helm after we cleaned up the boat, and took us fifty miles through some really clean and pretty water to about Mile #381RDB where I misdirected her into a state park marina not on the charts.

After she finished lecturing me on the necessity of accurate navigation, I was allowed to take the wheel and run us about four miles to Mile # 378RDB and into Goose Pond Marina at about noon. The sun glared unimpaired and the temperature could best be described as "hot as the hinges on the entrance door to hell". Fuel was priced at a very reasonable $1.589 per gallon and seven bags of ice sold for $1.25 each. The attendant was very polite and efficient and helped us push our boat around to the other side of the dock to have access to the waste pump-out system and fresh water to refill our thirty-gallon tank.

A serious leak has developed in the water system, and Spencer had tightened a leaking drain valve on the hot water heater to stop one leak. Apparently another serious leak exists somewhere else because in one day we were losing about twenty gallons of the thirty gallons in our tank. There is a state park here, a boat repair facility, and nice restrooms with showers which are close by the fuel dock.

In some areas Guntersville Lake has large patches of a

water-loving plant that grows from the bottom to the top of the lake surface in shallow areas. This provides good fish habitat but is a real problem for boaters. If an unlucky boater should stray into a patch of this green vegetation, his propeller(s) will wind it around the blades until no blades are visible. Then the boat will have no propulsion! There he will be with a bale of hay instead of a propeller. Goose Pond Marina has an on-going operation to remove the vegetation from the entrance channel by use of a machine that harvests the green vegetation from a floating barge. One must not stray from the marked channel into this unforgiving forest of floating greens for, if you do, there you will stay!

The sun beat down on us without mercy while we loaded fuel and supplies at Goose Pond. It made me think of the line from *The Rhyme of the Ancient Mariner* that goes, " Water, water, everywhere- oh how the boards did shrink; water, water everywhere and not a drop to drink".

Perspiration painted dark patterns on our clothes and there was no shade on the fuel dock and no shelter anywhere near. Hot and hungry, we went out the channel through the "greenery" to the main lake and anchored. Lunch was served and wolfed down and contrary to Mother's warning, "don't swim for thirty minutes after eating", Spencer and Carolyn jumped in the water to cool off. I tied a fender to a length of line and let it float behind the anchored boat in the swift current. The lake is a mile wide here, but the current is quite swift and the outdrive collects pieces of the floating vegetation as it drifts by. The water is clear and clean looking, and the floating pieces of vegetation go by only infrequently. Carolyn and Spencer clung to the floating line, as I did when I went in to cool off. Saundra didn't want to get in the water, and we couldn't coax her into swimming with us.

After our cooling swim we hoisted our anchor and cruised down Guntersville Lake through wide expanses of open water for several miles. Our destination was an island on the starboard side at Mile #352RDB. As the city of Guntersville appeared off our port quarter, a strong storm seemed to be forming behind us, and it was moving toward us faster than we were cruising. The storm soon covered the sky above our craft, and lightning twisted in angry ribbons that seemed attached to the earth at our stern. To say I was filled with anxiety is a slight understatement for we were the only craft afloat in a wide section of the lake. As we approached Goat Island a sheet of rain appeared to be following our progress, and a strong wind began kicking up small, white-capped wavelets on the surface. At this point it was a full-blown race against the storm and the throttle was pushed forward until the tachometer needle reached the red numbers. All four barrels of the carburetor were wide open and pulling fuel at an alarming rate. None of that mattered, only getting anchored behind the island was important. The run from Guntersville to Goat Island is about six miles, and each one seemed to take forever to cover, but we arrived at our destination ahead of the main storm.

We entered Honeycomb Creek and quickly found a spot just off the leeward side of Goat Island and dropped anchor just as the first of the large raindrops began to fall. I set the anchor hard by running the engine in reverse until the bow platform dipped and the boat stopped. By the time Spencer and I could get into the cabin, the strong thunderstorm arrived.

The anchor held fast as we were hit with very strong and gusty winds. The rocky shoreline was within thirty yards when we swung on the anchor and we were very glad the anchor flukes had found solid purchase below. Lightning soon was flashing in an arc of 360 degrees around us, but there were no close strikes. Trees on the island bent and swayed wildly as the wind gusts played across them like invisible hands stroking their limbs. A refreshing coolness encompassed us as though we had just walked into an air-conditioned house. A crisp, refreshing breeze swept the heat from inside the cabin leaving it a comfortable, dry haven from the raging thunderstorm outside. The concern for the lightning flashes and the thunderous booms that followed could be seen in the eyes of the two ladies and, I have to admit, I wished that we had less metal in our Bimini top, and that the radio antenna was a little shorter. Four support straps that secure the front of the Bimini top began to sing as they vibrated in the strong wind. The storm passed in about thirty minutes, but gave us only a few drops of water.

Turkey burgers were on the menu and on the grill soon after the storm front passed. As I was elected to be the chef today, I grilled turkey burgers for the main dish. Dinner was very g-o-o-o-o-d tonight, and the cool air and pretty location added to the atmosphere. Sleep came easily in the cooler air, but at about midnight I awoke to hear the wind playing a familiar song in the Bimini straps again, and could feel the boat swinging hard against her anchor line.

## June 5, 2002

Goat Island, Tennessee
Mile # 352RDB
To
Joe Wheeler State Park Marina
Mile # 277RDB.

Wednesday arrived cool and bright. We slept well and everyone seemed rested. After breakfast Spencer was casting a shallow running plug toward the rocky shore, thinking that was a good place for a bass to be hiding. Sure enough, he got a strike and soon landed a 14 lb. channel catfish!

Everyone was surprised and excited. Carolyn got her camera to record the event and was standing in the middle of the cockpit when the catfish jerked out of Spencer's hand and landed with a thud on the deck. It was wriggling and flopping and spreading blood around the white fiberglass deck. Carolyn shrieked, and launched herself onto the transom of the boat and held onto a support pipe for the Bimini top, with her bare feet in the air yelling, "Spencer, get that thing!" I thought surely she would fall in the lake. The hairline fracture in her foot apparently is no problem when she's in a panic! I'm sure Spencer will be boasting about this fish for a long time. He finally got the fish under control and we weighed and filmed it, then released it virtually unhurt. Carolyn, however, was still clinging to the support rod on the transom. I still can't figure how she got up there so quickly.

Spencer will be thinking about that big fish for a long time.

This is a wonderful place to anchor in daytime or at night. The island cove is well protected by the high trees of the island and the surrounding hills. It has two entrances and is immediately adjacent to the main lake, only three miles from Guntersville Dam.

It was June sixth at eleven in the morning when we hoisted anchor without trouble, and proceeded through the Guntersville Lock without delay. Wheeler Lake was clear of debris and was very scenic from the start. Spencer and I shared the piloting and navigating duties until we anchored at 12:30 just past the Redstone Arsenal Complex on Mile #327RDB. We fished while Saundra and Caroline prepared a lunch of salad, cold cuts and egg salad sandwiches. It was all very good.

When lunch was finished and the boat readied for cruising, we tried to hoist the anchor. It didn't budge. That's when all those stories about lost anchors flashed before my eyes. I didn't know what we were attached to, but it took us twenty minutes to free ourselves using Spencer's strong arms and the boat's engine. When we were finally loose, all I could think of was *Free at last, free at last, thank God a'mighty, free at last!*. Away we went, scooting along the water at a smooth but fairly fast clip toward the Brickyard Landing Marina in Decatur, Alabama. We had to wait for 20 minutes for the Southern Railroad lift bridge to be raised in Decatur because a train was going over it when we arrived. We weren't impressed with the store at Brickyard Landing Marina, and the advertised waste pump-out was nonexistent. This made Saundra very unhappy. Fuel was $1.799.

Decatur, AL lies on a wide stretch of lake and has many working towboats and we saw some of them in action. After leaving Decatur, we found ourselves cruising in wide, wide water toward Joe Wheeler State Park Marina at Mile # 277RDB. We topped off our fuel tank, pumped out waste, unloaded trash, and got fresh water and ice. This is a wonderful facility and I consider stopping here a pleasure. It has a great lodge with a restaurant and friendly service. The transient slips are free of charge and the docks and facilities are excellent. The attendant was exceptionally good and very friendly. Gas was $1.679 per gallon. We went past the marina and into the cove to a point about a half-mile above the marina, anchored and barbecued pork shops for dinner.

A storm seemed to be brewing so we decided to return to the marina and spend the night at the transient dock. We can use the air-conditioned showers and rest rooms and enjoy the security afforded by the park system of Alabama.

## June 6, 2002

Joe Wheeler State Park
Mile # 277RDB.
To
Mile #217RDB

Thursday we took advantage of the showers at Joe Wheeler State Park Marina, and they felt very refreshing. By nine o'clock we were ready to depart for Wheeler Lock. It took fifteen minutes for the lockmaster to prepare the lock for us. Once inside, things went well and we were out very soon. Wilson Lake was seventeen miles of beautiful water with no floating debris, no logs and no trash of any kind. When we arrived at Wilson Lock, we waited forty-five minutes for a barge to clear the lock before the lockmaster told us to enter. It was a ninety-three foot drop to Pickwick Lake.

Yesterday the weather was cool and today it's the same, with overcast skies. As we left the lock and started down the narrow channel toward Florence, Alabama, it began to sprinkle, then rained hard enough to run us off the fly bridge and to the lower station. It showered lightly for about ten minutes as we idled out of the canal and past the marina, as well as the park and recreation area on the shore to starboard. I polled the crew, and all voted to continue on to the waterfall at Cooper Hollow, Mile #217LDB, and have a late lunch. The wind increased, and we ran through the resulting white-capped waves for the next twenty-five miles.

We pulled into Cooper Hollow and anchored close to the waterfall. We barbecued pork chops again and they were delicious, as usual.

Several young people arrived and proceeded to dive from the falls, or dropped from a rope swing attached to a tree above the falls. As one boatload of youngsters arrived, one of them called to us and announced that they were out of control. We just cheered them on! They didn't stay long, probably because it was getting a bit chilly with the breeze, and we soon had the place to ourselves.

Saundra and I had been here before and stayed overnight on the sandbar at the end of the cove. This time, we stayed anchored close to the falls and enjoyed the sound of falling water. Spencer and I swam in the calm water of the cove while the whitecaps danced outside on the main lake. We had a cool breeze, strong at times, as we swam to the shale bar at the mouth of the cove. We went to bed in our sweat suits for the first time and slept very soundly. At mile 217, we're only two miles from the entrance to the Tenn-Tom waterway.

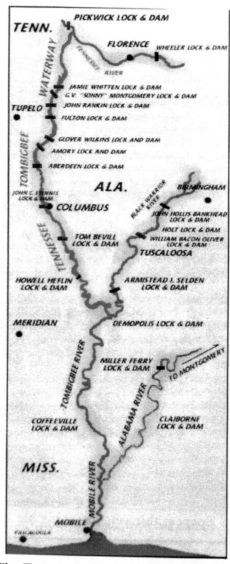

The Tennessee-Tombigbee Waterway
"The Tenn-Tom"

## June 7, 2002

Mile #217 RBD
To
Smithville Marina
Mile # 376.3LDB

Friday is cold and foggy at seven o'clock in the morning. The temperature is sixty-four degrees. By midmorning preparations are made for leaving Cooper Hollow waterfall. Since this is the first time any of us have entered the Tenn-Tom, we idled the three miles to Aqua Yacht Harbor where we topped off our fuel tank, took on water and ice and pumped out our waste system. The pump-out system had unbelievable suction and emptied our tank with dispatch. I thought it might collapse the holding tank. If anyone had been sitting on the head they might have been sucked through the plumbing.

The two young men on the fuel dock were very professional and helpful. Fuel was very expensive, $1.899, the most expensive to date.

Once we were out of the *No Wake* zone, we headed to starboard of the island at the head of the Tenn-Tom, then into the waterway.

Our run through the approximately 24 miles of the canal section called *the cut* went well, and we anchored for lunch at Mile #419.8R, across from the Crows Nest Public Boat Ramp. It was really too shallow, but we kept the out drive raised and were okay. A fisherman and his two sons stopped by to see if we were having trouble. They were very nice and we thanked them for their concern, finished lunch and continued through Whitten, Montgomery, Rankin and Fulton locks to the Smithville Marina just above Wilkins Lock at Mile #376.3LDB. As we approached the marina we wandered just outside the line of the channel markers and the propeller touched bottom. I think we're okay, so we continue to the transient dock where we are met by the owner, Jesse, who handles our dock lines, and his very friendly female Golden Retriever.

It was obvious that Smithville Marina had just been blessed with a significant Mayfly hatch. They covered nearly all the light posts and vertical supports near the transient dock with a fuzzy blanket of wings and antenna.

The golden retriever standing there looked odd, and Carolyn pointed out the fact that the dog had no hair on her belly. In fact her belly looked as black as ebony. We thought perhaps the heat had caused the hair loss but we can't figure out why the skin is black. Her tail wagged and she waited patiently to be petted. Jesse's family owned the land over which the marina is built long before it was flooded. He knows where the hog lot, cornfield and barn were located. The marina is built directly over the old hog lot.

This marina is showing its age and many of the floating slips are barely safe to walk on. The plastic, honeycombed units are disintegrating, and plywood is being added over the decaying material. Saundra and Carolyn are afraid to walk on the shaky floating dock to get from the boat to the shore. Smithville Marina is in need of major structural repair.

Smithville Marina is a friendly place with mostly older boats and houseboats in rental slips. Jesse is as friendly and helpful as anyone I have ever met. The permanent guests here are friendly, too. We had barbecued chicken for dinner with a vegetable tray for dipping followed by some really good coffee. A large trawler, *The Blue Moon*, tied up behind us. It was heading to Knoxville, Tennessee from Stewart, Florida.

Spencer was fishing from the dock when a snake swam under the pier he was standing on. He reeled the jig he was using to the end of his rod, and when the snake reappeared from under the pier he slapped at it, and the hook stuck just behind the snake's head. It instantly coiled tightly around the tip of the rod and there it stayed. Now what? He held the snake and rod tip underwater but the snake didn't seem to be inclined to drown quickly.

We might still be waiting for the snake to drown had not a lady noticed what was happening and come over to save the snake. She held it while I cut the hook with a pair of diagonal wire cutters.

The snake was released over the water, where it immediately dived into the water and disappeared really fast. A fourteen pound catfish and now a snake! What will Spencer catch next? A 'gator?

## June 8, 2002

Smithville Marina
Mile # 376.3LDB
To
Columbus Marina

Saturday is a breezy and refreshing morning at Smithville Marina. Saundra and Caroline took the courtesy car, a 1987 Chrysler, to Wal-Mart for supplies.

Saundra, Carolyn and Spencer Provisioning the *Saundra Kay*

Spencer and I are in charge of cooking all the meat left in the cooler after more than five days on the water. We are done by noon and still no sign of the ladies. I talked to Debbie, one of the full time slip holders here, and we all were invited to dine with her and the other permanent guests of the Smithville Marina in their Chapel. They are holding a dinner to honor Father and Mother's day. We had to decline because we planned to continue down the waterway this evening.

A large cruiser named *Chasing Dreams* came in for fuel and tied at the fuel dock. During fueling, the gas hose popped out of the filler hole. Gas spurted into the air, across the face of the owner of *Chasing Dreams,* and into his eyes. Jesse was drenched with gasoline from his waist to his feet. E-911 was called, and soon the place was full of flashing blue lights. The medics treated the man for his eye injury and soon transported him to the local hospital.

Fred Meyers, author of The Tenn-Tom Nitty-Gritty Cruise Guide, stopped by to see Jesse. He gave us some new information about possible problems ahead, which were not yet in the guide. We decided to continue on down the waterway at the strong urging of Saundra.

So, we left Smithville Marina, Gasoline $1.559, and were out of Wilkins Lock by five p.m. We locked through Amory and Aberdeen and arrived at Columbus Marina near the Stennis Lock at seven p.m. local time. We were tied up, plugged in, and secure within minutes of arrival in this very new and modern marina. We were positioned behind a large trawler style cruiser from Galveston, Texas, *The Ragged Edge.* Her captain and his wife were very nice people. They had a small dog on board, a Pomeranian. We slept well here in this new and very comfortable marina. We appreciated the professional staff too and the air-conditioned showers. Sunday morning is warming up, and the skies could best be described as "undecided".

## June 9, 2002

Columbus Marina
to
Marina Cove Marina, near Bevill Lock

On Sunday, Columbus Marina is left in our wake as we head to the Stennis Lock at ten o'clock and exit at ten forty-five. We expect to lock through three locks today and right now it looks good. But at Mile # 314.0 our propeller seems to spin in the hub and forward momentum is lost. The engine accelerates, but the boat doesn't move forward. Thinking that we may have picked up some grass or other debris around the propeller, we idle to the edge of the channel and anchor. I raised the out drive, and inspected the propeller for damage or anything that would explain the problem. Nothing was found that would explain the lack of propulsion. With the anchor back on board we tried to idle forward and found that we could move at about 1,200 RPM, or idle speed. So we did the only thing we could do in this situation and that was to idle for the next six miles to Bevill Lock where we radioed Marina Cove Marina. Permission was given to tie to the transient dock to make repairs.

We tied up at about 1:15 p.m. and decided to stay the night at the transient dock and tour the Corps of Engineers Tom Bevill Resource Management and Visitors Center. It is a southern style mansion near the lock, available for public tours. The stern wheel snag boat, *Montgomery,* is moored nearby but not open for tours.

The operator of Marina Cove is Fred Ellis, a friendly and laid-back man who is sympathetic and very helpful.

*Fred & Elma Ellis*
Proprietors

595 Marina Parkway
Carrollton AL 35447

## Marina Cove

Deep Water Harbor & Campground
Tenn-Tom Mile 307.4

Telephone 205-373-6701          Fax 205-373-2090
Cell Phone 205-310-6701          mymarina2@aol.com

USCG Licensed Yacht Delivery Available

While we prepared for dinner on the boat the *Dream Chaser* tied up on the transient dock.

The man who got gasoline in his eyes at Smithville was doing well, and they are continuing toward Mobile Bay. Soon another yacht arrived, fueled and tied to the transient dock. It was the *Irish Bandits* on an up-bound cruise. They had struck a submerged object just below Bevill Lock and damaged a propeller. At about dark a diver arrived with his helper and soon the diver was under the boat inspecting the propeller and found that it had to be replaced. While he was under the boat a snake, attracted by the light, surprised the diver. He came to the surface with a yell, and made sure the snake left before he went back under the boat. The diving operation was still underway when we turned in for the night.

## June 10, 2002

Marina Cove Marina
To
Demopolis Yacht Basin

Monday I am up at six a.m., enjoying the cool and quiet morning. Both large cruisers are still tied up at the transient dock. We must be about 485 miles from home and here we sit in the ass end of nowhere with something wrong with our boat. We'll try to change the propeller and check the shift linkage ourselves, then panic and look for professional help. This is the beginning of our eighth day on the water.

I tried to call the Bayliner help line number listed in the owner's manual but didn't get through. We borrowed a 1-7/16 inch deep socket from Fred Ellis and backed the boat onto a concrete ramp where we were able to raise the out drive, remove the old propeller, and replace it with my spare. The locking washer had spun out and the nut was loose. It's a miracle that the propeller had not been lost altogether. The rubber hub inside the propeller housing seemed to have been spun out and allowed the slippage we felt when we tried to accelerate. This should fix the problem, and we'll try to get the propeller repaired further down the waterway. It is 10:27 in the morning at the Marina Cove Dock and we are fueled and ready to load ice and move on south.

Soon the Tom Bevill Lock is behind us and the propeller

seems to be working well. The Gainesville Lock and Dam (Heflin Lock) at Mile #266.1 is soon behind us too and our luck seems to be holding. Starting at about mile #249 RDB through Mile #233 RDB the most scenic river bluffs were on the right bank. Tall, majestic, and white as chalk, with the sun shining against them. Several pictures were taken and Saundra pointed out one formation, which, at least to her, resembled Dolly Parton's chest.

Looking south on the Tenn-Tom Waterway just below Demopolis Lock and Dam

The mouth of the Black Warrior River at Mile # 217 LDB lets us know we're near Demopolis, halfway down the Tenn-Tom waterway, and soon the yellow pylons of Demopolis Yacht Basin come into view. These distinctive and tall, perhaps fifteen feet high, steel pipes are grouped together so they look like giant frames for tepees, and are spaced several feet apart. Barges tie to this line of metal pilings; this allows them to ride there in even the highest flood.

Advised by a friendly voice on channel 16 to turn to port around the farthest pylon, and avoid the shallow water across the pool where the boat ramp could be seen, our slow approach to the fuel dock was soon accomplished. A black gentleman who had spent several years in the U.S. Navy took our lines and demonstrated his knowledge of line handling. It was easy to tell by his jolly tone and wide smile that he loves his work here. Soon we were fueled, pumped-out, iced, watered, freed of our bag of trash, assigned a slip and tied up alongside the *Sea Curity*, a trawler waiting for a transmission to be repaired. The man and woman aboard helped us tie up and were very helpful. Spencer and I went exploring while the ladies checked out the facilities and the washer and dryer rooms and showers.

The Demopolis Yacht Basin lies in a cove, or basin, and is a large facility with a long, hinged walkway from the high bank overlooking the slips, to the floating walkways below.

You feel as though you are on a bridge over the water as you trudge your way up to the crest of the steep bank. There are no steps, just anti-skid material over the fairly steep incline of the walkway with rails on both sides. At the top is a two-story building containing a waiting room on the first floor under the washer, dryer, and restrooms above. A TV and many magazines, newspapers and books are there to keep you entertained while the laundry is being done. The waiting room is cooled by window air conditioners, but the washroom could only be described as a heated torture chamber. Only a small fan in the far wall tries to pull cooling air through the long room past the hot dryers, washing machines, unisex shower and toilet, without discernable success. I noted that one dryer exhaust vent pipe was disconnected from its through-wall fitting and allowed lint and heated air to blow into the room. This was reported as a potential fire hazard to a member of the maintenance staff.

A boat repair building and main office is to the left of the ramp. A short walk around the perimeter of the basin will bring you to the New Orleans Restaurant. High on a pier supported deck, perched well above the basin, and ringed by a covered veranda, it provides an excellent view of the basin and beyond.

A man who lives aboard his boat, the *Fast Eddy*, a Chris Craft of some size, came down the dock and asked where we came from, and we got into a conversation. Fast Eddy was tall, had unkempt hair and a goatee. His bare midriff showed a massive scar running across his lower stomach to a point halfway around his back. Another scar intersected with the longer scar toward his right side. The scars distorted his normal abdominal anatomy so that his belly button was drawn off center by two inches. As he talked, he had a nervous twitch that manifested itself in rapid arm movements, which took his hands to his head, shoulders, back and face. The more he talked, the more he twitched.

He told us of the various problems he had experienced with his boat, including shaft replacement and damage from underwater obstructions. At the moment he is laid up here, pending repairs to his boat. Knoxville and Morgan County, TN are his home territory. The only thing Fast Eddy didn't have to complete his unusual appearance was a parrot, a wooden leg and a jug of rum. He was familiar with Blue Springs Marina and had nothing good to say about their repair work. He told us about one of his ex-wives who was a druggist who kept him in a drug-induced coma for four years. Fast Eddy exemplifies one of the reasons long range cruising is so interesting because where else can one go to be

154

so entertained by stories home-spun while you wait, and by such colorful and interesting people? We excused ourselves and headed for the restaurant overlooking the dock.

Saundra enjoying coffee in the Demopolis Yacht Basin
With the New Orleans Restaurant in the background

When we walked into the New Orleans Restaurant, a gent seated at the bar just inside the door took a look at us and said to Spencer, "Hey man, you'll have to get a shirt on!"

His name was Chuck and I told him we just arrived and that we'd be back later for dinner. He said the food was very good. We went back to the boat and got freshened up.

Spencer donned a shirt, and we all had a delightful dinner at the New Orleans Restaurant. The food was good and the crowd was in a loud and boisterous mood. Even the air conditioning equipment, which must have been running on the lowest temperature setting, couldn't put a chill on the mood. The weather has been hot in the daytime with a blistering sun, but so far, the nights have been reasonably pleasant and cool. We've had no significant amount of rainfall since we left Tennessee although many fierce looking clouds have caused us to expect the worst. Today we had blue skies again, with wispy clouds to the west.

As we left the restaurant to return to our boat we met the captain of *Dream Chaser*, the same man who we'd met at Smithville Marina. He had the keys to the courtesy van that we needed to use the next day to get groceries.

In the morning we found it to finally be a wet day with showers falling steadily and hard at times. The night watchman asked for the van keys and explained that there was a two-hour time limit on the keys to the van. A lady had the van out at that time by using the spare set of keys, so we made arrangements to get the van when it returned.

Laundry was done and groceries were bought and delivered after the van was returned by a lady who had cut her foot and used the van to make a trip to the local hospital. Carolyn and Saundra made their way to a Wal-Mart store and found sleeveless shirts to help relieve the stress of the heat. Spencer and I finished the laundry while the ladies were gone.

We then took the damaged propeller to the repair shop and laid it on the counter. The man standing behind the counter took a careful look at the propeller as I described what had happened to us and what I thought was wrong with it. He fumbled through some very large books on the counter, and finally determined the part number for the propeller, checked his inventory and reported that he had none in stock but that he could order one. I asked about repairing the propeller and again a lot of looking through books and charts produced an answer. A gentleman who had been sitting behind the counter observing said, without rising from his comfortable chair, it could be repaired but cautioned me that there was a 50/50 chance that this model of propeller (Mercruiser Bravo II outdrive) would be broken during the rehubbing process. He suggested that I purchase a stainless steel prop instead for about $700.00. I figured that he just wanted to sell an expensive propeller so I had them send the propeller to a repair facility and have it forwarded and held for me at Dog River Marina on Mobile Bay. It cost $189.00 up front, but we needed a spare propeller. If it breaks, I'm out the money anyhow.

After the ladies returned, we decided to leave our slip at the Demopolis Yacht Basin and anchor two miles down the waterway on the port side. Fueled, pumped-out and with a supply of ice we left at 5:30 p.m. and cruised to a narrow channel on the port side of the Tenn-Tom about two miles from the marina, and about a mile upstream from the next lock. Carefully entering the mouth of Fosque Creek at idle speed we cleared the shallow entrance and steered close to the port side of the channel where the depth was about eight feet. Just a few hundred yards later we were abreast of the mooring station for the U.S. Coast Guard cutter *Wedge*.

When we went beyond and slowly turned to find the deepest water, the bottom of the boat touched ground. I raised the out drive, slowly backed off the obstruction, and moved us to a position directly across from the mooring station where Spencer dropped the anchor.

We grilled dinner on the trusty Magma Barbecue Grill and swam in the very warm but refreshing water of the quiet lagoon. Only one bass boat entered our watery hideout during the evening, otherwise we had our own private anchorage. This anchorage was across from a wooded public park. We watched a lady clad in a long, black dress walking to the edge of the park with a sketch pad or notebook in her hand. She appeared to be making notes or sketches of the bushes along the waterway, or something that was in their branches.

Spencer and I took turns casting lures toward the low, grassy shore but to no avail. This evening we all felt the weight of the rainy day and, encouraged by the arrival of a few mosquitoes, by the time darkness fell we were fast asleep. Our deep sleep was uninterrupted this night.

# June 12 2002

Fosque Creek
To
Alabama River cutoff at Mile # 52.8 LDB.

Wednesday is another early start. Up at six o'clock, we are anxious to get to Bobby's Fish Camp today, and to Mobile Bay tomorrow. The weather report forecast no rain for either day, but Friday calls for thunderstorms. This has been a good anchorage, but look out for shallow water if you go past the *No Wake* buoy at the end of the barge tie-up. The sky is clear this morning and everything is wet with dew.

After breakfast we hoisted the anchor and idled to the Demopolis Lock and Dam at Mile #213.2. At this point in 1979, the water rose to a record level of 72.4 feet, or 59.4 feet above the normal pool level of 13 feet. Only the red and green light fixtures were left above the flooding waters. The water is a cool blue-green color now, and thankfully it is at normal pool level.

When the lockmaster was contacted, he instructed us to wait for an approaching barge, and said he would let us go in behind the barge. We had a thirty-minute wait until the barge, *Judson B*, arrived and was tied in the lock. Once we were in the lock I could stand up on the fly bridge and see a cascading waterfall to starboard of the lock, where the water was falling from the spillway and over a wide boulder-strewn spillway several hundred yards across. It was spectacular. We were allowed to exit the lock at 8:25 a.m., ahead of the *Judson B*, so I was able to get a good view and take some pictures of this unusual scene. Several brave men were fishing from small boats next to the rocks.

The ninety-eight miles to Bobby's Fish Camp was covered without any major problem. Here we met Flint, the Native American dockhand, who said that Bobby fires him, or he quits, at least once every week. "Mr. Bobby", as Flint called him, was not the easiest man in the world to work for.

Two extra above-decks, five-gallon tanks of gasoline were loaded as insurance against fuel shortages for the next leg of the trip. Dog River Marina, located just ten miles south of Mobile, Alabama, lies off Mobile Bay on the western shore and is about one hundred and thirty miles distant.

Using my old-fashioned but trusty Canon 135MM, I tried to get some photographs of the cascading water as we left the lock. The morning sun shining in the east gave a strong backlight to the scene and made it difficult to record on film. The next six miles on the waterway were very scenic, with smooth rounded rock banks to the waterline.

They were about ten feet tall and appeared to have been worn down into the bedrock by the river in its relentless march to the sea over eons past. Sometimes the starboard bank would be solid rock and the port side would be soil, then for a distance, the arrangement would reverse. Sometimes, for a short distance, both banks would consist of smooth, solid rock. It gave the impression that it could have been made of poured concrete, finished to a moist smoothness.

At Mile 116.6, we entered the Coffeeville Lock and tied on the starboard wall, center bollard, across from an open boat. The *White Whale* was her name and she appeared to be about twenty-two feet long and made of aluminum. She had no top covering, no windshield and was powered by an outboard engine. The three men were bound for Panama City, FL on a deep-sea fishing expedition. We chatted with them for a while, and they seemed quite friendly and not at all concerned that their craft might seem small for such a trip. They were getting five and a half miles to the gallon of fuel, and had enough on board to get them to their destination. I have a feeling they will spend tonight in Panama City; about one hundred-fifty miles distant.

While we were in the Coffeeville Lock, we spotted a length of heavy hawser floating ahead of us in some debris. I contacted the lockmaster and told him we would try to pick it up as we left the lock. He looked and saw the floating line and thanked us for taking it aboard. I was afraid that it could get caught on our propeller, and what a job it would be to get it off! Once the gates opened and the other boat had exited, Spencer was able to snag the line with a boat hook and bring it aboard. He piled it neatly on the foredeck and we left the last lock on the down-bound run to Mobile Bay in high spirits.

We met a dredge and several barges, fishing boats and campers on the sandy beaches that lined the shore. These kept us to a slower pace since we had to deal with each situation carefully to avoid injury to property, people and feelings. A large boat carrying a car and a small boat met us in this section. Many sections of the waterway had floating debris, logs and limbs which we had to pick our way through. But we made 165 miles today and anchored near a moss draped tree about 800 feet up the Alabama River cutoff at Mile # 52.8 LDB. Saundra was quite concerned about camping under the tree. She had heard tales of cottonmouth moccasins, a local poisonous snake, falling from trees into boats. Her imagination took it from there. We made sure we were not directly under the tree, and that we would not swing under the tree if we were to swing on the anchor.

Carolyn prepared a late but delicious dinner. A cool salad with everything! It has been a very hot and humid evening, and at bedtime it still is very warm. The three 12-Volt fans in the cabin and forward V berth are our only relief, and without them we would have melted in the heat. Mosquitoes started to bite and we darted into the cabin and dropped the screen over the hatch. Our sleep was interrupted by a boat's wake during the early hours of the night, but nobody saw the boat. We slept well enough.

During the night the heat seemed to overcome the efforts of the small fans. The boat was very hot and I awoke covered with perspiration. Though I had only a light cotton sheet over my legs, it was too much. And there was something on my leg, probably Saundra's foot, I thought. So I started to toss the sheet aside when the weight on my leg moved in a way that made me know it could not be Saundra's foot. My heart leaped into my throat and I froze in place. There was only a slight, gliding movement against my leg, but my breath came with great effort now, my lungs straining to make no noise as I only took in enough oxygen to keep me from passing out in terror. The perspiration on my body was now a torrent, but my focus was entirely on the weight on my leg! My pulse was racing, and I wondered if my heart could stand the strain. The last thing I wanted to do was to wake the sleeping crew and cause a total panic in the darkness under the spreading moss-covered oak tree. Another movement was starting, moving up, up over the sheet and toward my torso. I panicked at that moment and grabbed my pillow from under my head to cover the unseen, slithering beast in a desperate effort to gain control of the situation. The pillow was raised slowly over my head, then brought down onto the unseen, wriggling mass with all the strength I had! The pillow pressing down made the outline of the wriggling, hissing beast felt against the inside of my thigh and its flicking tongue grazed my cheek. I flung myself against the bulkhead and as my eyes passed the open window of the cabin I saw the silhouette of the moss draping from the tree-directly over the boat. "Oh, S---!" I screamed at the top of my lungs, but no sound escaped my lips.

That's when I heard it; Saundra's soft voice saying, "Are you okay?" What a relief, only a nightmare. "Sure, just dreaming," I said. I wondered if this could really happen.

# June 13, 2002

Alabama River cutoff at Mile # 52.8 LDB.
To
Dog River Marina

Thursday is cool at 6:00 a.m., and the sun is still not up. The humidity is heavy in the air and we are all anxious to see Mobile Bay today. After all, this is our eleventh day on the water. The tidal effect is very visible here and it is obvious that the water level has fallen during the night by almost two feet. There's still plenty of water under us, about eight feet. Local fishermen going up the Alabama River cutoff idled by us with their fishing tackle hanging over the gunwales of their outboard fishing boats. They greeted us in a friendly manner and advised us to be cautious and check the depth carefully when we leave. Our location turned out to be perfect as an anchorage. We are still in the same spot and are still parallel with the shoreline near the moss-draped tree.

By eight o'clock breakfast was finished, our fine china cleaned and stored - that is to say that the paper plates and cups and plastic spoons were placed in the trash container - and by eight-twenty we had hoisted the anchor. There was a dead tree snag at the edge of the river just upstream of our anchorage so it became the perfect place to hang the pile of hawser that we had carried from the Coffeeville Lock. Spencer made the toss after I eased the boat against the snag.

It should hang there for a long time before the next flood takes it on downstream. Maybe it will just hang there forever, as a monument to our passage.

We were back on the waterway by eight-thirty, and noticed that it still had some floating wood. When we arrived at the north end of the twelve-mile island split, we noticed that from here the waterway became narrower, more like a river, and had a lot of curves, floating logs, and limbs.

Dredging operations on the Waterway are constantly removing shoals of sand. The curvy sections have many sandy beaches that reach out into the channel. It's the water vs Corps of Engineers every day. So far it seems to be a draw.

When the skyline of Mobile came into view, we were surprised to see many more floating logs and limbs. We had to be very careful to get through without damaging our propeller, so we just ran at idle speed all the way through Mobile, AL. It was a relief to see Mobile especially since after making the right-hand turn above Twelve-Mile Island. We saw no buoys or markers to indicate our location. In fact, we stopped and asked two factory workers on the shore where we were. "Tenn-Tom," they replied. "Just go that way and you'll run right into Mobile."

Mobile is a shipping center and it is obvious, as there is a lot of barge activity on both sides of the Mobile River.

Looking south on the Tenn-Tom Waterway at the entrance to Mobile, Alabama. This is a busy international shipping port on the Gulf Coast. Ships of all sizes are here, including a giant cruise liner in dry dock for repairs.

A large Carnival Cruise Line ship *Celebrity* is here in dry dock and she is very impressive as we idle by. The U.S. Navy had a ship here being worked on, and other ships were here being loaded or unloaded. It becomes obvious that Mobile is an important port with world class shipping operations. As if to say that Mobile has a lighter side, *The Cotton Blossom,* a stern wheel passenger boat, is moored on the downtown riverside.

At this point we have cruised approximately eight hundred and twenty-five miles and locked through eighteen locks, averaging a drop of forty-one feet each from a level of seven hundred and thirty-five feet elevation to sea level at

Mobile, AL. Our travels have taken us through Watts Bar, Chickamauga, Nickajack, Guntersville, Wheeler, and Pickwick Lakes and the entire length of the Tenn-Tom Waterway. The *Saundra Kay* has suffered only one spun-out propeller and a leak in her freshwater system.

After we left Mobile, AL and were out on Mobile Bay's shipping channel, our speed could increase to about 3,600 RPM. Soon buoy number 65 was reached and we turned west into the Dog River Channel. About two miles later we idled into Dog River on the west shore of Mobile Bay. There are marinas on either side and a few hundred yards further is our destination, Dog River Marina.

*The Dog River Marina*

We fueled, got water and ice, pumped out our waste tank then tied up in covered slip number 41. It was shallow, but there is 30 amp power and fresh water and we made it in at high tide. Yes, we are in salty water now and are out of the river system. It felt good to get out from under the scorching sun and in a breezy location. Soon the breeze got still and it got much warmer. Spencer has been working on his tan on the way down and he is starting to look rather brown. Carolyn, too, is a light nutmeg color. Saundra is slightly tanned on her shoulders and arms but I am the perpetual lobster shade of red. My freckles are darkening but the spaces between are sensitive and always red. I am using lots of sunscreen but sometimes I get forgetful and pay for it with sunburn.

The staff at Dog River Marina is very courteous and friendly. They made our stay here special. Rest rooms were good, and the washers and dryers are handy, and on the ground floor. A courtesy car was made available and we drove to Nan Sea's Restaurant on the shore and had a very good seafood dinner while enjoying a great view of the bay. Back at the boat the breeze had totally stopped with the sunset and it got much warmer. Sleep was slow to come and felt good. Saundra and I got up and sat on deck chairs in the cockpit to cool off at midnight.

The tide was out and the *Saundra Kay* was sitting in the muck on the bottom. The tide would have to lift us out of here.

# June 14, 2002

Dog River Marina
to
Fairhope, Alabama

On Friday the tide lifted us off the bottom by mid-morning. After breakfast, Spencer and I checked the batteries and found they were very low on water. It took five quarts of water to fill the two deep-cycle batteries. The heat in the engine compartment and heavy use of the batteries evaporates the water rapidly.

It will be hot today, so we decided to cross Mobile Bay to visit the city of Fairhope, Alabama - a city on the eastern shore with a population of over 12,000. This is a highly recommended stopover point on the bay. Another bag of ice is added to the already overfilled cooler, and we set out across the bay, following the Dog River Channel to the shipping fairway, then a heading of 125 degrees toward Fairhope, AL.

Mobile Bay has waves of one to two feet and we are able to cruise at a comfortable clip until we come into view of the channel markers. Spencer uses his binoculars to locate landmarks shown on our maps. The harbor is protected behind barriers that help keep waves to a minimum in the marina. It is called the Fairhope Municipal Pier, and is open to the public for fishing, jogging, walking or just accessing the open water. Lots of kids fish from this pier and we were happy to see teenagers doing something to entertain themselves besides listening to rap music or playing video games. The water in the bay is shallow, probably on average about ten feet, but much shallower in places.

We tied up alongside a trawler and went into Fairhope and had lunch at the ice cream parlor. As our walking tour took us through many small shops, storm clouds were forming over the bay and it became obvious that a strong storm was coming soon. Hurrying back to the boat, Spencer and I added mooring lines to better hold the boat. Waves were blowing over the break-wall and walkway by the boat. We closed the forward hatch, including the windows and the windshield cover - which was clinging by one snap - was reinstalled. It had been nearly blown into the water.

Rain pelted us as we went to meet Saundra and Carolyn under the shelter of the pavilion by the Yardarm Restaurant. Lightning flashed in blinding ribbons of superheated ionized air and thunder roared as the high-voltage flashes came raging down in terrifying splendor. Carolyn and Saundra seemed to cringe each time the lightning flashed and thunder echoed off the wall beside us. Strong gusts of wind whipped the water in the bay into a white, foaming pool of brine. In only about twenty minutes the storm subsided and it quickly calmed.

Our dinner in the Yardarm restaurant on the pier was very good, and the absence of the storm made it seem even more so. We watched from our corner table as the boats tied in their slips rocked and tugged against their restraining mooring lines, until they finally lay calm in their assigned spaces.

The Yardarm Restaurant in Fairhope, Alabama

The evening breeze from the bay gave a cooling finality to the day. It promised to be a most comfortable night, although we could still feel the small, choppy waves moving under our boat as we lay in our bunks, waiting for sleep to remove even that annoyance.

It is difficult to describe Fairhope, Alabama, in terms which will not seem an exaggeration. My best attempt is - simply beautiful. When you arrive from Mobile Bay you are greeted by the sight of a large water fountain encircled by a low concrete wall and planted with many varieties of roses. Benches are positioned for resting tired feet and to give a view of the bay. A large public beach is to the left, and large homes are nestled in live oaks on the right. They sweep up a fairly steep grade to the main part of town.

Everyone seemed to be very happy to be living here. Visitors are often invited to move here too. It is refreshing to walk through the streets and among the people of Fairhope.

Bill and Saundra on the beautiful waterfront and municipal pier in Fairhope, Alabama

## June 15, 2002

Fairhope, Alabama
to
Dauphin Island

Fairhope finds us still under her spell on Saturday, June fifteenth. The crew of the *Saundra Kay* is awake at 6:15 a.m., well rested after a cool and breezy night. A steady breeze from the north is blowing through the cabin door and out the forward hatch. It was a very good night's sleep! The sky is clear blue and the 1,400-foot concrete pier is busy with joggers and walkers taking their morning constitutional. It was nearly 8:30 before we finished breakfast. Our milk had finally soured and I had my cereal dry with fruit and coffee. Saundra was okay, but Carolyn was becoming affected by the wind and wave action on the boat. She was seasick after twelve days on the boat? She went ashore for a while and sat on the bench by the water fountain while Spencer and I took a walk into town.

The cooling breeze and the shade of the live oaks along the streets made it very pleasant. We brought back milk, bananas and muffins from the Muffin Man, fresh tomatoes, cheese, lunchmeat and four ears of fresh corn. And yes, we've been eating very well! Last night we dined in the Yardarm Restaurant on the municipal pier. Seafood is the main fare, and we agreed it should be rated 'Good'. The crew met and decided to go to Dauphin Island Marina at the western mouth of the bay after lunch today. Dauphin Island is one of a string of islands that divide the bay from the Gulf of Mexico. Shove off will be about 1:00 o'clock since the ladies are taking a nap now (12 noon).

Before we could get started, the wind began to build and white capped waves danced on the bay. The crew all agreed to wait for the waves to calm down after talking to the captain of the trawler in the slip next to us. His trawler, large enough to live aboard, however, was not large enough to comfortably travel across the bay in these conditions. He advised us to wait until the wave height and wind subsided.

I gladly took his advice and laid on my bunk and let the waves rock me to sleep. When I awoke it was 2:30 p.m. and the bay had calmed considerably. The decision now was to make a run to Dauphin Island and by 3:30 we were under way. It was a nice cruise of about an hour on rolling seas with the boat occasionally leaping off a high wave and into a trough, throwing spray all around! I like these conditions as long as there is no real danger to the boat. It was a following sea with a strong breeze on our backs, so we threw a lot of spray but everyone enjoyed the ride. A bulk freighter was going down the shipping lane, so we crossed astern and passed an oil-drilling platform before entering the channel to Dauphin Island Marina. It required a three-mile no-wake speed through a shallow, winding channel in front of many large and elegant beach homes.

The hot afternoon sun was too low on the horizon for the Bimini top to give us any shade so the sun took her revenge during the trip to the Marina fuel dock. The attendant tied us to the fuel dock alongside the marina office at 6:00 p.m. The dock-master said there would be a band playing on the dock beside us till 10:00 p.m., celebrating the end of a fishing rodeo. The band was called *Joe Right and the Naked Gunmen.* We were in a party mood so we said – OKAY!

Dinner was at the Boats restaurant, which had a seafood menu! Carolyn was really feeding her craving for shrimp. This island is ideally suited and situated to be a sport-fishing center. Numerous charter boats are working out of here, and we inspect their large catches of snapper and other desirable fish. The men are working hard to fillet the fish. It is illegal to dump carcasses into the sea here, and we watched a Japanese restaurant operator take the carcasses away. We're told it will be made into fish soup stock and the like. It's good that it doesn't go to waste. The people are easy to talk to, and one lady gladly explains the procedure for going on a charter.

At about 7:00 p.m., a trio started playing music on the pier in front of the bait shop and played until about 8:00 p.m. When the celebration was ready, the *Joe Right and the Naked Gunmen* Band started playing on the dock right in front of our boat.

Everyone, about a hundred, was invited to eat the crawfish, corn and fish which was laid out on benches along the pier. The music was fairly loud and beer was a necessary supplement for the revelers to lubricate the crawfish on the way down. At first it was interesting to watch the party and the music was not bad. Once, three or four men were seen aside from the rest of the party talking about some type of disagreement, but no fights happened.

One man, they said the one who organized the party, became convinced that he was a gifted dancer and was dancing around by himself, totally out of time with the music. And to add to the silliness he was white, had no rhythm and was wearing a giant sombrero. AND, he kept it up until nearly midnight! Quitting by ten? Oh, yeah – right. It was midnight when they finally turned the amplifiers off. What a relief!

# June 16, 2002

Dauphin Island
to
Biloxi, Mississippi

On Sunday, the dock looked like a major party bomb had exploded and covered the dock with beer cans, crawfish shells, and other trash. Two huge rolling garbage containers were overflowing with empty beer cans. At five a.m. the charter boats are getting ready to go out, preparing bait and other supplies before the customers arrived.

I took a Styrofoam bucket to the bait house and bought two dozen shrimp. The supply of shrimp was nearly gone already. The bait shrimp boat was already dragging the bottom of the protected area outside the marina for more bait shrimp. This morning promised a bright, sunny day with high, thin clouds around the horizon. Weather predictions for today are for scattered thunderstorms. By 8:00 a.m. the party mess was completely cleaned up, and the last party boat has gone out to fish. After breakfast on the boat, Spencer and I showered and got the boat fueled and ready to go to Biloxi, MS. Late in the morning the *Saundra Kay* made her way out of the channel and under the Dauphin Island Bridge, into the Mississippi Sound.

Our heading was 270 degrees (West) as we followed the Inter-coastal Waterway toward Biloxi. Our charts were easy to understand, but I found it difficult to identify some of the markers, and to locate others. I knew that it was important to avoid shallow water, and the best way is to stay in the marked channels. I used the compass to navigate between markers. The water was pretty and we expected a two-hour run to the Biloxi Small Craft Harbor near the Beaux Rivage Casino. I had called the casino long before the start of this cruise to get familiar with the location of the marina.

Everything seemed to be going pretty well until I realized that we were too close to the south shore of Round Island and in shallow water. Too late, I felt the propeller touch the bottom. I raised the out drive and carefully idled back into deeper water. When I accelerated, the boat seemed to take a very long time to get back on plane, and once on plane, I decided to run without stopping for Biloxi Small Craft Harbor Marina. It was likely some damage was done to the propeller, and as long as we could run I felt we were that much farther ahead.

As we approached what I thought was the first buoy on the entrance of the channel to Biloxi, we slowed to verify our location with a fisherman anchored nearby. I slowed, went to neutral gear, and to completely stop, I put the engine into reverse gear. The sound of the engine left no doubt that our propeller had just spun off. It was 12:45 p.m. local time.

Spencer inspected the raised out drive and verified my suspicions. There was no propeller, hub, locking washer or nut! Just then, over the VHF Marine Radio, a Coast Guard weather warning began. It advised all boats in the area to head for port immediately, for all passengers to wear life vests, and for vessels unable to get to safe harbor to drop safety anchors and take precautions to ride out a severe squall line heading this way. Everyone donned their life jackets and wondered what could happen next. We were in sight of the Biloxi skyline a short distance away. What a time to be without Depends! Spencer dropped our anchor and I got on the radio and requested assistance from any boats in the area. Two boats were visible and neither answered my call. Finally, a reply from Sea Tow Service was received. Sea Tow fixed my position from the numbers I got from the buoy and the description of the skyline I was able to give. Now we had to wait!

As it turned out, Sea Tow showed up at 1:30 that afternoon and took us in a stern-to-bow tow, and headed directly toward Biloxi following the channel markers.

It took about an hour and a quarter to get to the entrance of the marina where he took us in an *alongside* towing position. It was not easy to get us headed into a slip, but he did it and no damage was done to our boat. Although the terrible squall line never materialized except for a cooling shower, and Sea Tow charged us $225.00 for his services, the crew of the *Saundra Kay* was glad and relieved. And no, I didn't have towing insurance. We were safely in slip #2, and the harbormaster was most helpful and sympathetic to our situation. He allowed us to stay, without charge, for the first two nights. The regular rate for a slip such as the one we are in, is $27.50 per day. We were in a first class marina in a coastal city, which is a vacation destination, within walking distance of excellent restaurants, gaming Casinos, beaches and saltwater fishing. I had a spare propeller, the one rehubbed, forwarded from Demopolis to Dog River, but no locking washer, outer hub or nut.

The emotional state of the crew is gloomy and depressed. There is open discussion of returning home without delay. Spencer reminded us that New Orleans holds no special attraction for him. Biloxi is within sight of the tallest buildings in Gulfport to the west. New Orleans is not far beyond, perhaps an hour's drive by car. This would have been an excellent time for a rousing and inspiring speech by the captain to rally his crew. I could think of nothing inspiring to say.

Across the street from the marina office is a McDonalds Restaurant. We had sandwiches for a late lunch/early dinner and took a walking tour of our immediate area. It is a beautiful place and right on the Mississippi Sound. One can look right out onto the Gulf and watch shrimp boats, charter boats, and pleasure boats going about their business.

Many large charter boats work out of this harbor and shrimp boats are moored here too, but in a separate section of the harbor. Later in the evening we met Ken Smith, the owner of a 28-foot boat called *B.B.B. Boat,* moored in slip #5.

We explained our situation and he offered to help us in any way he could. He even offered to have his wife take Saundra and Carolyn to the grocery store if they needed to go shopping. We gratefully accepted his help and made plans to meet him the next morning to go looking for the exotic parts my boat needs to install our spare propeller. He also explained the obvious; the name of his boat is *B.B.B. Boat* because Ken has a stutter. This night we slept soundly in the cooler sea breeze, and perhaps partly because Ken has given us what we all need, hope and a plan! The air was cool enough to make a sweatshirt feel good.

# June 17, 2002

## Biloxi, Mississippi

This morning, Monday June 17th, Saundra and I enjoyed a delicious breakfast at McElroy's, a restaurant here in the marina complex. Carolyn and Spencer ate at McDonalds. We were back at our boat when Ken arrived at about-nine thirty and took Spencer and me to Ross Marine Propeller, a propeller repair shop in Biloxi. They sold us a hub but didn't have the lock washer or nut in stock. They did provide us with the correct part numbers for the items we needed, including the number for a proper replacement propeller.

It was easy to see by the large numbers of propellers on the floor waiting to be repaired that I was only one of many who have suffered from the shallow water in the gulf. The gentleman also called other marinas and found the parts we needed. We went to another boat dealer at Rivers Bend Marina in Gulfport and purchased the locking nut and washer, the only ones he had in stock. Apparently the Mercruiser Bravo II outdrive is a rare unit and few parts are sold for it. Total cost of the parts was about $62.00.

We were unable to make arrangements for anyone to replace the propeller for us so we did it ourselves. Lying on our stomachs on the swim platform, we were able to reach the raised outdrive. Using a special socket designed for replacing water heater elements, we were able to install the spare propeller while still tied in our slip. It took us longer to accomplish because we were very careful not to drop any part into the deep water under our boat. The socket worked, but we were unable to torque the nut as much as we would have liked. By noon the installation was completed and we were sea worthy again. We plan to check the tightness of the nut after we run the engine for a half-hour or so.

While we were in the boat repair mood, we decided to change the engine oil and oil filter. I used the hand pump to remove the oil and pump it into an empty water jug. The marina has an oil tank for recycling used oil and a dumpster for disposal of trash. I am constantly pleased to learn of the services and convenience afforded by this marina.

Everyone has been wonderful to us here, especially Ann and Ken Smith.

Ken Smith and his *B-B-B Boat*
*In the background is the marina office building, restrooms, and showers*

Ann took the ladies shopping yesterday afternoon, so we now have provisions aboard to start the return leg of this cruise when we get ready. We had lunch at the Seafood Harbor, a restaurant here in the marina complex beside the shrimp boat mooring slips. We walked past a Vietnamese lady selling fresh shrimp off the family shrimp boat near the restaurant.

In the late afternoon we walked to the Visitors Center across the street from the marina. The two hostesses were very knowledgeable and helpful. We learned of the local area, and were assisted in arranging for a rental car from Swifty Rentals, for a trip into New Orleans tomorrow. The cost for the rental car was $49.00 per day, and that included delivery and pick-up of the car.

Carolyn purchased some shrimp to use as bait, and Spencer and I fished over the seawall and caught many small catfish, Spencer caught an eel and I pulled a nice flounder to the surface before it broke my fishing line. The sea breeze was brisk and the water was choppy, but we were using large sinkers. We fished until well after dark.

This evening we had a dinner of rotisserie chicken, baked beans and onions. There was serious concern expressed due to the fact that no Beano was aboard! We decided to trust in the sea breeze instead. As I drift off into a sound sleep I am excited about going into New Orleans tomorrow.

## June 18th, 2002

Biloxi, Mississippi
to
New Orleans, Louisiana
(And back to Biloxi ... by rental car)

Tuesday, June 18th arrived and the usual sky conditions were clearly visible; clouds were forming on the horizon and a steady cool breeze was coming from the Gulf. The weather prediction is the same one we've heard often. That is, "Possible thunderstorms and temperatures in the high 90's".

Perfect for street surfing in New Orleans, The Big Easy! We met Steve Schreider from Swifty Car Rental and took the mid-sized sedan via the scenic Route 90 along the coast; through and beyond Gulfport to New Orleans, where we parked in the Harrah's self-park garage, across the street from the casino. Carolyn had been elected to drive into the city, and I agreed to drive the return trip. We went into the casino and Carolyn and Saundra played slot machines for enough time to get our parking ticket validated so our parking was free.

Our tour of New Orleans included walking around the French Quarter, lunch at Johnny Armstrong's Restaurant, and a trolley ride on the St. Charles trolley from Canal Street through a section of the city along Jackson Blvd, where many beautiful homes line the street. I took pictures of many of the ones I thought were exceptional examples of residential architecture. We were surprised when the conductor, a large black gentleman, called loudly, "End of the line-everybody off"! We had to exit the car and re-board and re-pay our fare of $1.25 each. The conductor simply walked to the opposite end of the coach and drove it back to Canal Street. It was a noisy ride but a very nice way to get the flavor of that part of New Orleans, and when a quick shower came, it was an opportune shelter from the rain. Back on Canal Street the weather was clear again.

It was apparent that Spencer was not especially interested in New Orleans and was going along to please the others in the group. Carolyn appeared somewhat interested and Saundra was not exactly thrilled with the whole thing. So I gave up on my effort to be tour guide and we all headed back to the car in Harrah's garage.

I drove on the return trip and I must say that the signs that lead you back to the Route 10 east ramp suddenly disappear just before you can get onto the highway. We wandered and finally did the unthinkable, asked a local for directions. Soon we were on the highway back to Biloxi. It was late and we hadn't eaten dinner. Saundra seemed to be having a problem with her sugar level (she's a diabetic). It was dark when we got back to the boat and ate dinner. A vote was taken and the decision made to begin our return trip toward Tennessee tomorrow, if the sea conditions are right.

Spencer didn't really enjoy New Orleans and Saundra was tired. I wondered if they were all getting homesick. After all, we are nearly nine hundred miles from home, and have been on this boat for sixteen days! That's a lot of togetherness on a twenty-five foot boat!

## June 19, 2002

### Biloxi, Mississippi

Today is a pretty day with some large, puffy clouds and one low, gray cloud that showered us first thing in the morning. We will prepare to leave soon. The *hours* meter on the boat reads 427.2 hours. We started with 367 hours on the engine, so on the way to Biloxi we ran the boat engine a total of 60 hours (running and idling combined), covering 900 miles and 18 locks. That represents about fourteen percent of the total lifetime usage of the boat in nine seasons. We will check all the systems of the boat before we head to Dog River Marina on the western shore of Mobile Bay, near Mobile, Alabama.

Ken Smith, our helpful new friend, had his wife check the local weather report and it was not good. Wave conditions were two to three feet with a 15-knot wind from the south. That would have been rough sailing during an easterly run in our boat, so we decided to stay another day hoping for better seas. We spent the day doing nothing much but relaxing. Spencer and I tried to find a socket to fit the propeller nut but couldn't locate one. We filled our fuel tank for the return trip and enjoyed the pleasant day.

# June 20, 2002

Biloxi, Mississippi
to
Dog River Marina.

Thursday finds us up at five-thirty, so we can get ready and leave early to take advantage of the calm water of the early morning. By six-thirty we are in the channel out of Biloxi, MS. We were careful to stay in the channel this time, but the weather began to build as we headed eastward on the Inter-coastal. It became difficult to stay on course because of the wave height (2-3 feet), and the distance between markers. It got really rough and we had difficulty in making any speed. When we tried to plane on the top of the waves it really gave the boat a beating. The ladies were doing okay in the cabin, but Spencer and I were hanging on tight on the fly bridge.

Most of the way we were heading into an easterly wind, which did help. The compass would swing wildly, and I could only take a reading by interpolating the average reading. But the sun was visible through thin clouds to the east so once I had my bearing I simply used the sun to keep on course. The critical turn around Round Island was easy because I was able to follow the path a barge took to the key buoy.

During the run toward Round Island, the girls handed up some miniature cupcakes for a snack. When I tried to eat one it fell apart and the gooey crumbs went everywhere. I then tried to drink some coke from a can, but it spilled down my shirtfront.

When the image of the Dauphin Island Bridge came into view, there was no more need for navigational aids. We headed for the wide span of the bridge, passed under it and turned north east toward the ship channel into Mobile. The change in direction slowed our progress dramatically. The waves in the bay were more difficult to handle because of their spacing and size. When we reached the shipping channel, we changed our heading to due north. The wind-driven waves from the northeast kept pushing me to the western edge of the channel.

We finally arrived at the channel markers for Dog River, and soon were tied to the fuel dock at Dog River Marina. We had run five hours from Biloxi in rough water and needed a break. Carolyn informed us that her bladder had nearly burst while she waited for calmer water to use the marine head on board our boat.

After fueling and another great meal at Nan Sea's Restaurant, we made arrangements to stay overnight and have the boat hauled and the propeller checked in the morning. An underwater check by feel suggested that the propeller hub had seated itself, but the locking washer was loose under the nut. It will cost us $100.00 to have it inspected and tightened.

Spencer and I walked around the large shipyard and were amazed at the size of the boats and the scope of the work being done. A new yacht was being fitted out and was worth several million dollars.

Some boats were being completely painted and we noticed a large sailboat with a man on a ladder after working hours. He was carefully sanding the upper hull. He introduced himself as Charles Browder, the fifty-three year old retired brother of singer-entertainer T. J. Shepperd. The sailboat was the *Terrifying Witch*. She was about seventy feet long and her mainmast was fifty-five feet tall. Mr. Browder told us he had bought her at a government auction after she had been stored for twelve years. She had been taken by the government because of involvement in the drug trade, and he described her at that time as "all green inside." Forty-eight thousand cash was the auction price and he expects to have about one hundred thousand in the ship when it's finished.

His dream is to write songs and sail to all the blue water ports around the world. He doesn't want to challenge bad weather, he said, so his travels may be limited somewhat by the elements. Sailing with him will be his wife, dog, Siamese cat and macaw.

We wished the captain a fair wind, and we hope to see him and the *Terrifying Witch* in Nashville someday

Tonight we stay in shallow slip #41 again.

## June 21, 2002

### Dog River Marina

Friday at Dog River Marina is quiet. After showering I met Chip Lucas, owner of *Chips Ahoy*, a beautiful boat and quite large enough for him to live aboard. He is quite an experienced boater and loves his forty-one foot President. His stories of challenges on the Tenn-Tom are interesting and informative. He is dedicated to the proper care of his aging cat that suffers from diabetes and requires shots. Home port for him is at Lake Guntersville Mile #358.

Turner Marine actually did the hauling and inspection of our boat, and sure enough, the nut and washer were loose. I felt much better about paying the $100.00. Normal rates for hauling a boat here is seven dollars per foot or one hundred and seventy-five dollars for hauling us out. They were trying to help us out and we appreciated it. And, the marina didn't charge anything for our overnight stay in their slip. There was no problem with the tide this morning either.

## June 22, 2002

Dog River Marina
to
Choctaw National Wildlife Refuge
Mile #123.2 RDB.

By 8:20 the next morning we were idling out in the channel toward Mobile Bay ship channel. The water was very rough, so rather than risk a mutiny, or worse, I decided to maintain a slow pace through the upper bay and to a point above Mobile. This would put us into the Mobile River, the entry point of the Tenn-Tom system. There we resumed normal cruising speed and were pleased with the clarity of the water and the absence of debris, logs, chunks of wood and such.

At mile fifty-five the boat was running well and the miles were ticking off when, without any warning, a tremendous explosion and rattling sound was heard. Instantly two worried faces appeared in the cabin door below asking, "What was that"? Carolyn and Saundra thought the engine had exploded. The Bimini top over the fly bridge, now on its ninth season, had given in to the strain of the air pressure and the threads across the rear support had ripped completely across. The material was flapping wildly and making a lot of noise. After anchoring at the edge of the channel, we rolled up the flapping Bimini top and stored it in its storage sleeve. Then when Mile #78 was reached I noticed an alligator on the bank, perhaps six to eight feet long. The return trip is beginning to get interesting.

Spencer piloted for a large part of this stretch and I assisted by spotting potential trouble and handling the radio communications. By four p.m., Coffeeville Lock was reached and here was our first major delay. Tied to a mooring pier below the lock, we swung in the current and wind for about an hour before we could enter the lock after a barge emerged and headed south. Our fuel gauge read *empty* and why not? After all, we had been running for seven hours and forty minutes! We dumped the two above-deck supplemental five-gallon tanks into our main tank while we were waiting to get into the lock.

Once in the lock, we tied on the port side at the upstream end, because the lockmaster said it would be a better ride. Wrong! The in-rushing water spun the boat around and pinned the port bow rub rail against the wall. Caroline could not push it away from her position in the forward hatch. I went to help but had no better luck. After the flow slowed somewhat I got a fender between the bow and the lock wall.

Once out of the lock, we quickly cruised to Bobby's Fish Camp at Mile #118.9RDB. Flint, the Choctaw Indian dock hand was not there to meet us on the fuel dock, so we tied to the dock and allowed space for a large trawler following us to tie up near the pumps. I helped take their mooring lines when they pulled in. They seemed to be very nice people. The fish camp seemed nearly empty. Just one couple sat in the shade of a camper awning. In the store/restaurant people were eating dinner, and Flint and some women were managing the restaurant and store business. I told Flint we wanted to eat first and then fuel up. He said, " No problem".

Spencer and I decided to try the catfish dinner while Saundra and Carolyn ordered burgers and chicken. Everyone enjoyed the food, but we couldn't eat it all. Spencer said he had never seen anything like it. Slaw is the specialty of the house and is served while you are waiting for the main meal. Served family style, you can just help yourself as long as you like. We must have eaten a half-gallon of slaw.

As soon as we had eaten dinner we filled our tank with gasoline and headed upstream toward an anchorage about forty-five miles away. We were hardly out of the fish camp area when I narrowly missed a floating log due to the diminishing light. Our anchorage choice for the night changed to one within two miles of Bobby's Fish Camp at the Choctaw National Wildlife Refuge. Our anchors were dropped at the entrance of the Refuge, fore and aft. The entrance channel appears to be about two hundred feet across, but narrows to a tight curve at about four hundred yards from the entrance. The moon was high and full behind the stern of our boat and it was a pleasant evening. All of us were in our bunks by nine p.m.

How do we know Saturday, June 22nd has arrived? Because those d--- bass boats started zipping around us at 5:30 this morning, rocking the boat and waking everyone! Oh, well, coffee and breakfast is finished by 8:15 and a light shower is falling while we discuss our next move. Saundra, whose vision is acute when fear is present, claims she has spied a *school* of alligators on the shore. So far, they have not attacked.

Now that the rain has driven everyone into the cabin, my body is signaling me to go to the head to relieve myself.

Saundra has just announced that we should be able to cover 329 miles today; evidence of a deepening depression and a raging anti-river sentiment. Spencer said the crew is considering abandoning ship.

By late morning the drizzle has lessened and it appears to be clearing. Our anchorage at Okatuppa Creek/Choctaw National Wildlife Refuge has been very good at Mile #123.2RDB. By eleven the *Saundra Kay* is cruising toward Demopolis Yacht Basin at Mile # 216.1. The waterway is very clean of debris. Carolyn spotted an alligator on the shore as we cruised through almost perfect water. Few fishermen or campers are spotted, probably because of the rainy weather predicted for this weekend. But it's Saturday, and a few hardy souls are out there, like the fisherman who woke us this morning.

At about Mile #160, Spencer called my attention to the eastern shoreline where a large wild hog, apparently dead, lay on its side with a large black dog standing beside it. It didn't appear to be bloated, as it would be if it had been dead for a long time. It probably has recently been wounded and was able to make it to the water's edge.

Again Spencer and I shared the duties at the helm and by 2:45 we approached the Demopolis Lock. The lockmaster asked for registration information, while we waited downstream in the swift current as he prepared the lock. Once inside we waited while the crew changed shifts and the new lockmaster let us out. We idled most of the three miles to the marina dock, fueled, got ice, water and a pump-out then tied up in our old slip. The ladies took the courtesy van into town for supplies. We are thankful that the van is made available to us at no charge, but it is in need of major repairs. Every trip in it is an adventure and a successful return to the marina is cause for celebration. When they returned we ate dinner on the boat and ate too much, as usual. The sky was very cloudy and we were rained on heavily. Perfect timing again!

# June 23, 2002

Choctaw National Wildlife Refuge
Mile #123.2 RDB.
to
Columbus Marina, Mile #335 LDB

Awake at six in the morning on Sunday and ready to get started again! By seven-twenty Carolyn and Spencer are doing laundry and it's starting to rain again. Saundra announced that this is what boating is really all about - getting wet! Prospects for cruising north, or in any direction, don't look good right now. The marina is predictably inactive. I rigged a poncho over the forward hatch to allow for ventilation without rain coming into the v-berth. If the wind stays calm we'll be okay, if not, it's goodbye poncho-hello raindrops in the V-berth. Since there is no cover above the cabin door, the rain can fall right in, so I rigged a golf umbrella over the door. It works when the rain is falling straight down but Saundra said we have a *Mary Poppins* look.

The large trawler in the next slip is still here. *The Sea Curity* had her transmission repaired when we were here last, and now she is waiting for a new water pump. Boating =$$$. Waiting is a large part of boating too; waiting for locks to open, close, reopen, rain to stop, courtesy cars to become available, head to be empty, pump-outs, parts to arrive, towing services to arrive, trash to wash ashore, trips to start and trips to end.

Mostly boating is sharing time with special people who share a special appreciation of the lakes, streams and waterways. When all conditions are perfect, boating is the most pleasant activity I can imagine. When conditions are the worst, it is the most aggravating, costly and dangerous undertaking! We like it!

Wayne Fulmer was pulling his boat out of the fuel dock at Demopolis and heading for a slip to spend the night when I realized that our boats are alike. This is the first time in nine years I have seen a twin of our boat. I called out to Saundra to show her. Wayne stopped by our slip later, and told us how he and his wife enjoy their boat very much. I believe he said that his boat has a 351CID engine and is slow to plane out. Ours boat has a 454 CID or 7.4 Liter engine, and has no problem getting out of the hole as long as it is not grossly overloaded. He told me that there is another boat like ours in Columbus Marina and it has been modified to carry a diesel engine and a generator.

Wayne's boat's name is *Aqua Lady* and he is from the Birmingham area and boats mainly on the Black Warrior system. I promised to call him when I got home to tell him which size Bimini top I ordered and installed to cover the cockpit of our boat. He also said his wife prefers to sleep in the bottom bunk below water level. They have never used the V berth or the cabin berth.

At about eleven o'clock, Demopolis Yacht Basin is a pleasant memory and our next destination lies to the north. Skies are very cloudy and the crew has been openly plotting to speed up the return to that magical place called "home". High fives by Spencer and Saundra to a yell of "Yes!" can only be a bad omen. I think they have hatched a plot to get us into the Tennessee River System by running 118 miles, seven lockages, and *the cut* tomorrow.

At one p.m. showers chased us below, and I briefly used the lower station. The run through Bevill Lock was fine, but, from there to Stennis Lock was pure agony! By the time we got on plane a fisherman or a beach picnic group would cause us to have to go to idle, time and time again. Lots of people use this waterway on the weekends for family outings on the many beaches, and when the weather is right, fishermen take advantage of this well-known bass fishery.

I passed a barge and towboat that were parked against the bank and appeared to be inactive. As we cruised by I noticed a small skiff tied alongside the barge and a man walking there. About that time Spencer said, "The captain just motioned for us to slow down!" It was too late to lower our wake since we were almost past them by now. Just a little past the barge the captain hailed us on channel 16 and told me that they, the barges, don't go fast by small boats and I should treat them the same way. He also said that the skiff took quite a beating by our wake as did another small boat I never did see. I explained to him why I maintained speed and apologized for any problem I had caused, and that I would make sure it never happened again. How we missed seeing the skiff and the man on the barge I'll never know.

After the conversation with the barge captain, the luxury yacht, the 155 foot long *Liquidity* appeared ahead in the channel. The captain communicated his intentions to me by simply saying, "Port to port". Was I going to argue? No way! We idled by each other on the "one whistle". The boat, completely white, dwarfed our tiny craft. This section of the waterway has some very tight curves, and a constant vigilance must be kept in order to avoid the barge traffic and other commercial activities. Some curves are so tight that it is impossible to stay in deep water and keep our boat *on plane*. When we saw the front of a barge begin to appear around a tight bend in the river, we immediately took action to put the boat in a safe position; then contacted the barge captain to determine where he wanted us to meet him. There is no time to daydream in this section.

Spencer took the boat on to Stennis Lock, stopping at Marina Cove to take on fuel. Fred Ellis had raised his fuel prices considerably since we were here on the way south. He said business is slow and according to other marina operators on the waterway, it is slow everywhere. And to add to the difficulties, the Corps. of Engineers will close three locks for maintenance for three to four weeks soon. That should really slow things down. The lockages through Bevill and Stennis were very comfortable and easy on the boat.

At 6:30 p.m. Stennis Lock was behind us and the *Saundra Kay* tied up to the transient dock at Columbus Marina, Mile #335 LDB. This is a wonderful place with super service and attention from professionals. The bathrooms and showers are air conditioned, roomy and clean. This is a great place to lay over and use the pick-up truck to get provisions in nearby Columbus, Mississippi. That's what Spencer and Carolyn did this evening. The sky is very cloudy and lightning is dancing around the horizon in a 180-degree arc as we go to our bunks at 9:30.

## June 24, 2002

Columbus Marina, Mile #335 LDB
to
#218.7LDB (Bug Holler)

Monday at 6:00 a.m. It is a clear day. Yesterday's storm clouds are gone and the sun is bright and hot this morning. Some small, wispy clouds linger in a brilliant blue sky. The weather forecast is for 85 degrees and no rain for the next two days. We'll top off our gas tank, fill the two five-gallon above-deck tanks, and then cruise toward Tennessee waters. All this in order to prevent a mutiny!

Each of us showered and took advantage of the excellent facilities here at Columbus Marina. By 8:30 a.m. the *Saundra Kay* is cruising north on the waterway with a crew that is determined to be on the Tennessee River system by the end of this day. Saundra seems to place special value on accomplishing this. The vote is three to one, so we begin the quest. The waterway is now amazingly free of debris and there are almost no fishermen on the waterway. The locks are spaced close together now, and one lock in particular can be seen upon exiting the previous lock, a distance of approximately five miles away.

The lockmasters prepare the locks before we arrive in most cases, and we can idle right in and tie up. A large trawler called *Big Shoe* joined us in our northerly run at about the fifth lock. At 1:00 p.m., a brief shower drove us from the fly bridge and I used the lower station for a few minutes. The sky is clouded over, and rain is falling in sheets in the distance. Lightning makes us wonder whether we should stop. We fueled at Midway Marina, where we found the fuel priced at a delightful $1.449 per gallon, cheapest fuel on the whole cruise! We caught up with *Big Shoe* before the next lock and we locked through together. Inside the lock we talked with the captain, and discovered that he is bound for Nashville and "wherever". Since the next lock is about eight miles away, I told the captain we'd run ahead and tell the lockmaster that he is on his way and suggest that he hold the lock open for his arrival.

Once out of the lock we cruised ahead and arrived at the next lock, entered and tied up. *Big Shoe* had been really running hard, and arrived soon after us and went to the other side of the lock to tie up. The lockmaster closed the gates quickly and we were trapped inside the lock tied to a bollard by our center cleat.

*Big Shoe* must have been coming too fast because we were soon bouncing wildly as her wake rocked us for the next twenty minutes. For a while we thought that it would rip out our center cleat or break the 3/8-inch nylon line. It seemed that the bollard would rise as our boat fell on the wake, then reverse the process. I believe the wake was at least two feet high inside the lock. No damage was done to our boat largely because of the efforts of my crew. Strangely, there was no apology from the captain of *Big Shoe* or any comment from the lockmaster. I decided never to lock through any lock where *Big Shoe* is present. This lock is the Jamie Whitten - the last lock between us and the Tennessee River System. It will lift us eighty-three feet to the level of the water in Pickwick Lake.

As we exited Whitten Lock, a serious-looking storm loomed ominously to our southeast. Our decision to outrun the storm was another decision that could be debated at length. Suffice it to say that our effort was futile as large raindrops started to fall just before we were to enter the mouth of the 24-mile *cut*. Lightning danced in ever-nearer patterns and the booming thunder rattled our confidence.

Dense walls of falling rain were closing in on us from behind. I slowed, raised the out drive, and pulled the boat just off the buoyed channel and into shallow water. Our experiences with shallow water in the past three weeks have made me very leery of getting out of the marked channels.

Spencer dropped the anchor about one hundred feet off the channel in eight feet of water and we went into the cabin. Rain was falling and thunder and lightning did what it usually does in a strong afternoon storm in the heat of summer. About that time, a three-wide barge came out of the cut heading south. She took all the south side of the channel to line up for the next section. We're all glad we are here while he passes, instead of meeting him in the narrow cut during a thunderstorm.

In about twenty minutes the storm passed and the air got calm. We hoisted anchor and headed into *the cut*, cruising comfortably in the rain-cooled air. The next twenty-four miles are often described as a boring run in what is essentially a canal with riprapped banks on both sides. Actually, I found it to be refreshing. Partly because the water was clear, the air cool and we met only three fishing boats and one water-ski boat for the entire length of *the cut*. A few raindrops fell occasionally, but even those were refreshing.

Remember that we have no Bimini top on the fly bridge, and the sun has baked us for a long time. Cool and wet is good to us! By 4:00 p.m. we exited the waterway and entered the Tennessee River system in Pickwick Lake Mile #215.0. After anchoring in a cove at Mile #218.7LDB (Bug Holler), I barbecued pork chops on the magma grill and they were delicious. We spent the night in Bug Holler, and true to its name, we suffered a few mosquito bites. Can you say West Nile Virus?

# June 25, 2002

Columbus Marina, Mile #335 LDB
to
Joe Wheeler State Park Marina

Tuesday finds us up at 6:00 a.m. and having coffee. At 6:45 it started raining, a very slight, gentle shower out of a mix of patchy clouds and blue sky. The shower is brief, hardly worth the mention, and Bug Holler, as the locals call this cove, is quiet again. A bass boat glides to the bank at the mouth of our cove and its occupant starts tossing lures at the water's edge. After breakfast was finished, we cruised up the shore for two miles to Coleman State Park Marina, a newly renovated state facility with a lodge, cabins, and conference center. This is a pretty location, but there is no restaurant and it seems more geared to the permanent slip holders and renters of the cabins or lodge/convention center. But the layout and construction of the lodge is very good. Gas is sold for $1.909 per gallon, but no attendant was present on the fuel dock for at least thirty minutes. This is a very slow pace and why not? We emptied the two five gallon cans of gas into our tanks and headed out into Pickwick Lake.

The water is choppy at first, and has patches of floating debris and wood. Spencer took the wheel on the run to Wilson Lock. At Wilson Lock we have a few minutes wait then the ninety-three foot lift to Wilson Lake, and we're off to Wheeler Lock with Spencer still at the helm.

The water here is pretty choppy, but we keep cruising and when we rounded the point we called the lockmaster on channel 16. He said to come on up and be ready to enter the lock as soon as he cleared it, and gave us the green light. Little did we know that a barge was working in the lock and it would be forty-five minutes before we would be able to enter. We "wallered around", as the captain of the barge Yazoo City described it to the lockmaster. After forty-five minutes, we went into the lock behind the exiting towboat with fifteen barges in his tow.

We are soon on our way again, and this time for only about two miles to Joe Wheeler State Park Marina. This place is so very nice we decided to stay here on the way home, and take advantage of the restaurant in the lodge, the showers, free dockage and reasonable fuel prices. Funds for this park were authorized during the term of Governor Lurleen Wallace, and the park was completed during the term of Governor George Wallace of Alabama.

Our fuel tank and water tanks are filled, the waste tank emptied at the fuel dock. Our boat was allowed to stay tied there since there was "no business today", according to the dock master. The restaurant in the lodge was still serving lunch, so we rushed to get something to eat, as they close for an hour before they serve dinners. Grilled chicken breast and burgers were just what the doctor ordered for our crew. Delicious and at $5.95 a good buy!

Again, at seven in the evening, we went back for dinner and found that we still had an appetite. Spencer and I selected grilled quail and the ladies had prime rib of beef. All enjoyed their meals except Carolyn who found her prime rib to be too well done for her taste. I thought the quail was very good and enjoyed the meal very much. The service was good and the prices were reasonable. A salad bar was available and included items for dessert. The really nice touch is the dinner music in the background and the tall, wooden ceiling with massive beams and posts.

After we finished our dinner, we moved the boat from the fuel dock to the transient dock. Altogether, the experience at Joe Wheeler State Park Marina was just excellent!

## June 26, 2002

Joe Wheeler State Park Marina
to
Crow Creek Island at Mile # 401RDB

Today is Wednesday, and I am up at five-thirty; I take a walk to the public bathroom, around the shore to the lodge, and back. By then the crew is awake and it is six o'clock. The sky is sunny with just a few clouds. While we were eating our breakfast, a young man walking along the transient dock stopped by our boat and began a polite conversation.

He was about thirty-five to forty years old, six feet tall with dark hair and wearing sunglasses. His T-shirt had Rio Dulce, Guatemala printed on the front, and it naturally aroused our curiosity. He told us that his large cruiser was parked at the lodge where he was staying with his children, sixteen, eight and six years old. During our conversation, he described the paradise he had found in Rio Dulce, Guatemala, where the water, weather and morals are ideal. After his dissertation we knew why at least twelve brides jump two hundred feet from a bridge to their deaths each year still wearing their wedding gowns after their grooms found them not to be virginal. All this with an active, lava-spewing volcano in the background. And we now know that there is a reason why women go to the bathroom in pairs! A very interesting man!

After breakfast on the boat, we left Joe Wheeler State

Park Marina at about 8:10 a.m., with Spencer at the upper helm. After a twenty-minute wait for the Decatur, Alabama lift-bridge to clear a train, we still made it into the Guntersville Lock by noon. Our run up Wheeler Lake has been very smooth on water that, at times, looked like a mirror. The upper stretches have some high stone cliffs overlooking the water. Wheeler Lake is a very scenic lake.

Few fishermen were out, and only a very few pleasure craft were seen on the entire length of the lake. We've decided to stay at the Guntersville Municipal Marina at Guntersville, approximately nine miles upstream from the lock, so we can go ashore and purchase some steak or pork chops to barbecue tonight.

The lockmaster told us that heavy rain was moving across the lake toward the lock, so we covered the fly bridge and took shelter in the cabin. Thunder could be heard as the *Saundra Kay* left Guntersville Lock with Captain Bill at the lower station. From the lock to the Municipal Marina in Guntersville we were in a rainstorm, strong at times. Sheets of rainwater fell on us and flashes of lightning divided the sky into jagged sections. We began cruising with the windshield wipers slapping and my white-knuckled crew staring out fogged-up windows to catch a glimpse of a buoy, or any marker through the rain. It was serious business. When a buoy was spotted to port Saundra yelped with relief and pointed it out to me.

The intensity of the storm gradually diminished and our progress was good, considering the conditions. We arrived in Guntersville Municipal Marina just as the squall line passed and just before the next squall line struck at 1:00 p.m. A lady wearing a dress over a swimsuit met us on the dock and secured our mooring lines. She said she didn't mind getting wet as she tied us to the cleats by the fuel pumps.

Tied at the fuel dock, we were rained on again and a stiff wind tried to make it difficult for us. A cruiser came in behind us at the dock and I took their lines to help tie her off in the stiff wind. The code of conduct for boaters requires every hand to render aid when it is needed. It is always appreciated and will be returned many times over.

After the second squall had passed, we filled our fuel tank, bought a quart of oil for a spare and loaded two bags of ice into our cooler. Gasoline was $1.90 per gallon. This dock is a good facility and actually has a restroom near the gas pumps. A small office is there also. But the building on the shore where the office should be is in a shambles. The lady who met us on the dock was very helpful and allowed us to borrow a twenty-five year old pickup truck. Spencer and I finally got a chance to do the shopping. We managed to find four excellent New York strip steaks in a Foodland Grocery store in Guntersville. Tonight, we grill!!

Guntersville is a town that could be described as typical in the south inasmuch as it has a mix of old southern mansions and modern homes on the outskirts of town. The main road through town is a two-lane, one-way street separated by a city block. These two streets seem to be the only major streets in town. A sleepy town, it seems to be in no hurry. Even the traffic seems to be slower and the drivers less competitive or aggressive.

At four o'clock in the afternoon we left Guntersville and headed upstream to a spot behind Crow Creek Island at Mile #401RDB, our best anchorage of all. There was twenty feet of water under us, a strong breeze from the west and a strong current from the east. It was an almost even match between the effect of the wind and current with the breeze finally winning and pushing the stern around to a ninety-degree angle to the shore.

Spencer grilled the strip steaks to perfection on the Magma Kettle and after relaxing for a while, we found we were pleasantly exhausted. At nine o'clock, everyone went to bed. Carolyn was feeling better and was over her bout of motion sickness. However, she has never gotten her "sea legs," and when the boat rocks she is not at her best.

# June 27, 2002

Crow Creek Island at Mile # 401RDB
to
HOME at Mile 559.6RDB

This is to be the last day of this cruise, and I am up at six o'clock with high hopes of raising the anchor by seven. My crew has developed a bad case of the five hundred-yard stare or "get me home soon" blues. There's no current under us this morning, but we still have a slight breeze.

Apparently, the water release is not underway at Nickajack Lock and Dam. The sky is overcast with thick, gray clouds and no sunlight can get through. I took the fly bridge helm, and Spencer raised the anchor with no difficulty. We were off and cruising at seven fifteen a.m., our earliest start to date. By eight-thirty we are tied on the port wall of Nickajack Lock. The sky is growing more threatening now with low, gray, moisture-laden clouds. Our hope is to make it to Chattanooga before we get caught in another storm.

The crew is calculating the mileage to our home port and trying to convince me that we should make a run for it today. I expressed my opinion that Chattanooga deserves one more day before we finish this trip. When the votes were counted, I lost. Sometimes democracy sucks! For the next few miles the crew accused me of pouting. Imagine that, a grown man pouting just because he didn't get his way. Just because I was clenching my teeth and staring straight ahead and refusing to speak! They tried to console me by saying that we could do Chattanooga anytime by car. At nine-fifteen we stopped at Hale's Bar Marina, just above Nickajack Lock, to get fuel.

The water is green and the trees grow to the edge of the water line. This lake is very pretty here, and has sweeping panoramic views of tall stone bluffs and peaks. This section just below Chattanooga is called *The Gorge*; I read a water depth of over ninety feet in one place.

Raccoon Mountain, located just a few miles west of Chattanooga, still looks much the same as it did when Cherokee hunters stalked bear and wildcat there in the 1800's. It is still home to whitetail deer, woodchucks, gray foxes, a large wintering population of bald eagles and, of course, raccoons.

Today, an artificial reservoir holding over 12 billion gallons of water sits on the mountaintop. And deep below, hundreds of feet down in the heart of the mountain, are elevators, lighted tunnels and huge pieces of heavy machinery. It's not a Hollywood set for a new James Bond movie. It's TVA's Raccoon Mountain Pumped Storage Plant- now recognized as one of America's most outstanding engineering projects.

Scorned at the outset as a scheme worthy of Rube Goldberg, pumped-storage systems have since proven their value. Designed to operate like giant storage batteries, pumped-storage facilities require two water reservoirs, one located at a much higher elevation than the other. Energy is stored in the upper reservoir in the form of water. When this water is released to fall to the lower reservoir, the energy of motion is transferred to turbines attached to electric generators.

After careful study of the geology of Raccoon Mountain, TVA engineers concluded that a pumped-storage facility could be built at the site. Construction began in 1970. More Than 1,000 workers labored at Raccoon Mountain during the next several years, excavating 10 million cubic yards of earth to build the upper reservoir and sealing it with a huge 8,500 foot-long dam, the largest rock-fill dam ever built by TVA.

The project also involved digging 12,000 feet of subterranean tunnels, carving a space the size of a football field out of solid limestone, and installing four massive vertical-shaft, reversible-pump turbines.

Originally scheduled for completion in 1973, the Raccoon Mountain plant wasn't finished until 1979. The cost was about $300,000,000.00, but it worked well beyond all expectations. Water stored in the upper reservoir can provide twenty hours of continuous power generation during peak-demand hours and then can be pumped back up to the mountaintop during low-demand hours. The plant is also able to change power output rapidly, thus matching load and supply as well as providing a backup power source throughout the day.

It is this flexibility that makes Raccoon Mountain unique. It is designed for quick start-up. When extreme weather strikes or another plant shuts down, Raccoon Mountain is ready. In just a few minutes it can start producing electricity, and lots of it! Raccoon Mountain is a major factor in the efficient, reliable operation of the TVA power system. The only evidence of its existence on the Nickajack is a concrete structure on the right shore and an opening into the mountain in an area where no other evidence of human activity exists.

Ross's Landing Marina in Chattanooga appeared to starboard at ten-fifty a.m. Again nobody can be seen on the docks and there is no answer on channel 16. We pulled up to the fuel dock and tied. The fuel pump was turned on, so we filled our tank. Carolyn went to the office to pay for the fuel but had trouble locating the attendant. Finally, she found him and was able to complete the transaction. The restrooms were locked again and no key was available. The office rest rooms were made available for our use. They were very nicely decorated and thank goodness the plumbing worked. The office floor ceramic tile is still only half installed. What's going on here?

The crew definitely wants to press on to home port today so I reluctantly agreed, even though I do believe they would have enjoyed spending an afternoon and evening in downtown Chattanooga. At noon, we headed for the Chickamauga Lock only five miles away. When we arrived at the lock I received no response to my radio call. I repeated the call at fifteen-minute intervals and still there was no answer. I thought they might have an emergency or were very busy. It was very hot out there in the open with the sun boiling down. Finally we pulled up to the small craft pull-chain and gave it a yank. Soon an attendant came around the lock in a cart. About forty-five minutes after we arrived we were signaled to enter the lock.

Spencer took the helm about thirty miles from Watts Bar Lock. It rained on us for a few minutes at about four p.m., and I ran the boat from the lower station during the rain. The fly bridge got wet and the radio wouldn't work to call Watts-Bar Lock, so I gave a horn signal. By four-fifteen we were being lifted to the Watts Bar Lake level of 735 feet elevation above sea level.

The run on Chickamauga had been very pleasant. Green water with a slight chop for the first fifteen miles or so and hardly any other boats made it a special run. At four-thirty Watts Bar Lock is behind us as we head for home port, about thirty miles away. As I was leaving the lock, the lockmaster came over and verified that my radio wasn't working and gave me a pamphlet, which he said would be helpful to have on board. It was titled, "Locking Through". I did not need more information, just a dry radio, but I accepted his offering in the spirit in which it was given. I couldn't help it if my radio suddenly failed without warning. I piloted our boat to Blue Springs Marina where we pumped out the contents of our holding tank, but their office was closed, so we couldn't top off our fuel tank. We had arrived after their regular closing time. Spencer took the helm for the rest of the way home at Mile 559.6RDB.

We stopped briefly at our neighbor's dock to announce our return. We were home by six p.m. That means we've been running from seven-fifteen in the morning until six in the afternoon with an hour for lunch - that is a total of nine hours and forty-five minutes from Guntersville Lake Mile 401 to Watts Bar Mile 559.6,and through three locks. One hundred forty-eight miles is a long way on the lake system. Anyway, we are all home and happy and have a tale to tell about the *Trip of a Lifetime* - when we went down the Tennessee River on a chainsaw.

Unloading the boat on our dock was a final chore that really marked the end of the trip. It probably took forty-five minutes to get everything up to the house. It was obvious to us that we had traveled "heavily".

Spencer came over two days later to help clean the boat and store her under a tarp. We also changed her oil and oil filter. The trip from Biloxi amounted to the equivalent of 3,000 road miles in a car, so we figured she needed to have a fresh supply of oil after all that work. The final engine hour reading was 481.7 hours. 114.7 hours of running time was used to cover the nearly 1,800 miles round trip to Mobile Bay, the Gulf of Mexico, the Mississippi Sound and Biloxi, MS. Thirty-six lockages were made, one propeller was lost, we were towed to port, and one old fly bridge Bimini top was torn. But, best of all, no personal injuries were suffered by our crew. And yes, we did make it to New Orleans even if we had to cheat and use a rental car from Biloxi.

What does it feel like to go ashore after almost a month of life aboard a small boat with two good friends? I can speak for Saundra and me when I say that it seems odd to be on shore. Our home is modest, small actually, but we felt sort of lost in the roominess. All things are relative, I guess, and it took nearly a week before we felt "at home" again.

Saundra relaxing in her favorite rocking chair,
holding a life ring from our boat.

I took five rolls of film to the local Wal-Mart for developing and met my friend, Ray Buck, walking the main aisle. After a short chat, he asked me whether I would do it again and I said "No way. We saw it once going down and once coming back up, that's twice and that's enough for me". "Been there and done that, huh?" Ray responded.

Today is July 8, 2002 and at 7:25 a.m. I was standing on the outer edge of my deck overlooking Watts Bar Lake when I thought I heard an airplane coming down the lake. Small planes often fly low over this part of the lake, and sometimes we can watch them doing aerobatic maneuvers. But this time it was our new friends, Dave and Carol Anderson, in their 28-foot Wellcraft, heading out on their month-long cruise to New York. They passed our house and dock blowing the horn and waving back at me. I suddenly had the feeling that it would be so much fun to do another cruise, a totally different one to a new destination, somewhere we've never been! Maybe...

This log is submitted by

*Capt. Bill Gillum*
*July 8, 2002*

# About the Author

BJ Gillum was born and raised in rural Kentucky and never lived near a significant body of water. Is there any wonder that he developed a deep curiosity about the river and lake systems that virtually surrounded his home state?

He retired in 1994 after a thirty-five year career in the Bell Telephone System, the former Western Electric Company now called Alcatel-Lucent Technologies.

His boating career consisted of family camping trips to Dale Hollow Lake and Cumberland Lake in Tennessee where he fished, swam, and water skied with his wife Saundra and their sons.

A trip across Lake Erie in a deep-hulled ski boat was his only cruise of length until he retired and used their cruiser, the *Saundra Kay,* to travel to Kingston, Tennessee from sixty miles north of Pittsburgh, Pennsylvania.

Nearly ten years later he and Saundra took another long cruise, this time from their home on Watts Bar Lake, Tennessee, to New Orleans, Louisiana. These are the cruises described in this book.

"BJ" Gillum started his writing career in 2003 and has since authored six novels, including:

- *Alabama Rising – The Erectolite Affair*
- *King of the Kudzu*
- *The Reluctant Terrorist*
- *Best Seller List – A Dream to Die For*
- *Darwin's War*
- *Forget Me Not – Love's Never Long Enough*
- *Down The Rivers on a Chainsaw*

*All his titles are available on*

***Neilans.com***
***Or***
***Amazon.com***

Made in the USA
San Bernardino, CA
15 January 2017